PERGAMON INTERNATIONAL LIBRARY
of Science, Technology, Engineering and Social Studies

The 1000-volume original paperback library in aid of education, industrial training and the enjoyment of leisure

Publisher: Robert Maxwell, M.C.

CLINICAL UTILIZATION OF MICROCOMPUTER TECHNOLOGY

THE PERGAMON TEXTBOOK INSPECTION COPY SERVICE

An inspection copy of any book published in the Pergamon International Library will gladly be sent to academic staff without obligation for their consideration for course adoption or recommendation. Copies may be retained for a period of 60 days from receipt and returned if not suitable. When a particular title is adopted or recommended for adoption for class use and the recommendation results in a sale of 12 or more copies the inspection copy may be retained with our compliments. The Publishers will be pleased to receive suggestions for revised editions and new titles to be published in this important international Library.

Pergamon Titles of Related Interest

Barlow/Hayes/Nelson THE SCIENTIST PRACTITIONER:
Research and Accountability in Clinical and Educational Settings
Bellack/Hersen DICTIONARY OF BEHAVIOR
THERAPY TECHNIQUES
Nietzel/Dillehay PSYCHOLOGICAL CONSULTATION
IN THE COURTROOM
Pryzwansky/Wendt PSYCHOLOGY AS A PROFESSION:
Foundations of Practice

Related Journals*

CLINICAL PSYCHOLOGY REVIEW
COMPUTERS IN HUMAN BEHAVIOR

*Free sample copies available upon request

PSYCHOLOGY PRACTITIONER GUIDEBOOKS

EDITORS

Arnold P. Goldstein, Syracuse University
Leonard Krasner, SUNY at Stony Brook
Sol L. Garfield, Washington University

CLINICAL UTILIZATION OF MICROCOMPUTER TECHNOLOGY

RAYMOND G. ROMANCZYK
State University of New York at Binghamton

PERGAMON PRESS
New York   Oxford   Toronto   Sydney   Frankfurt

Pergamon Press Offices:

U.S.A.   Pergamon Press Inc., Maxwell House, Fairview Park,
                        Elmsford, New York 10523, U.S.A.

U.K.   Pergamon Press Ltd., Headington Hill Hall,
                        Oxford OX3 0BW, England

CANADA   Pergamon Press Canada Ltd., Suite 104, 150 Consumers Road,
                        Willowdale, Ontario M2J 1P9, Canada

AUSTRALIA   Pergamon Press (Aust.) Pty. Ltd., P.O. Box 544,
                        Potts Point, NSW 2011, Australia

FEDERAL REPUBLIC   Pergamon Press GmbH, Hammerweg 6,
OF GERMANY   D-6242 Kronberg-Taunus, Federal Republic of Germany

Library of Congress Cataloging in Publication Data

Romanczyk, Raymond G.
    Clinical utilization of microcomputer technology.

    (Psychology practitioner guidebooks)
    Bibliography: p.
    1. Clinical psychology--Data processing.
2. Psychology, Applied--Data processing.
3. Microcomputers. I. Title II. Series.
[DNLM: 1. Computers. 2. Professional Practice.
3. Psychology, Clinical. WM 26.5 R758c]
RC455.2.B38R66   1985   616.89′0068   85-12156
ISBN 0-08-031946-7
ISBN 0-08-031945-9 (pbk.)

Printed in Great Britain by A. Wheaton & Co. Ltd., Exeter

Contents

Preface

This guidebook is intended for the professional or student in clinical psychology, or related areas of human services, who is not acquainted with microcomputer technology. The motivation to write this book came from many years of providing advice and consultation to researchers, clinicians, educators, and administrators involved in the diverse field of psychology as well as related disciplines. It was always frustrating that there was no simple guide that could provide basic background information from which specific discussions could ensue. Thus, this guidebook is intended to be exactly that: a guide. It is not meant to be an exhaustive reference on all software and hardware currently available, nor is it intended to be an authoritative text on computer science.

Computer technology is changing at such a fast pace that a product or specific technology review quickly becomes outdated. Applications and needs do not become outdated as quickly and thus serve as the structure of this guidebook. Because the microcomputer is a multifaceted tool, each individual must engage in a process of self-assessment of need, and then examine and compare the hardware and software that is currently available. There are scores of word processors, data bases, accounting programs, statistical programs, and so on, and, except in rare instances, it would be a disservice to simply recommend brand A or brand B. This guidebook should serve as a starting point from which to begin the search for a microcomputer system that will meet individual needs.

I have also taken some liberty in presenting certain information in a somewhat simplified manner to achieve a conservative position. That is, for the sophisticated computer user, there are many modifications and alterations that can be performed to greatly enhance the operation of a given microcomputer. Skill and finesse can often make what seems to be an impossible task, possible. This is, however, not representative. Thus, I have taken the approach of presenting information from the perspective of the novice. Although a particular product or component could be altered or utilized in a nonstandard fashion by a skilled user, and since the novice would be unable to make this adjustment, to hold this out as the norm would be misleading. I have attempted to present a conservative overview, one that will, I hope, present no unwelcome surprises to the novice. As skill and experience of the user develops, the reward will be continued expansion of use and flexibility.

I have been fortunate over these past 10 years to have been associated with a number of individuals who have significantly assisted in my development of hardware and software skills. I would like to express my gratitude to Jerry Beauchamp, Kris Kafka, and Robert Soutner, and in particular to Wayne Kashinsky for his continued and extensive tutelage. I also wish to thank many of my current and former staff members and graduate students who supported my tinkering and assisted me in fully developing the systems I use today. These individuals include: Elissa Savrin, Dan Crimmins, Ellen Berler, Linda Matey, Gep Colletti, Nancy Ponzetti-Dyer, and especially Janet Kistner, Tony Plienis, and Stephanie Lockshin. A special thanks to Jeff Heath, a highly skilled programmer who often assists me in translating my ideas into functional software. I would also like to recognize the contribution of Bob Klepac, a friend and colleague who has so freely shared his expertise with me. I have had many enjoyable conversations with Bob that have helped crystalize many of my reflections on the interface between psychology and the microcomputer revolution. My sincere appreciation also to Roxanne Wells for her great skill and efficiency in the preparation of this manuscript and to Jerome Frank and Phyllis Hall of Pergamon Press for their support and enthusiasm for this project.

Introduction

Psychology as a science has had a wonderful and colorful history that is fascinating to study. Although one can trace an extremely long lineage of our profession, it is nevertheless reasonable to state that psychology as a science came into its own during the 19th century, produced a revolution in thought during the 20th century, and is following a pattern of acceleration. Much of psychology's development as a science revolved around the issue of measurement and quantification. It was the solid use of the scientific method that has permitted much of the growth and strength in the field.

It is thus interesting to also trace the history of computer technology. It too has a very long history with innumerable methods and devices that have been used to perform calculations for many centuries. However, as in psychology, the strongest roots are found in the 19th century with devices such as adding machines and automated looms. The 20th century brought rapid progress with the use of Hollerith cards and the invention of vacuum tubes and transistors, and currently we are witnessing an explosive growth in the area of computer science. The Mark I (Automatic Sequence Controlled Calculator), created at Harvard in 1939, marked the advent of the true computer, albeit in this case a mechanical one. The creation of ENIAC (Electronic Numerical Integrator and Calculator) in 1945 and UNIVAC (Universal Automatic Computer) in 1951 marked the beginning of the first generation of electronic computers (and unfortunately, also perhaps marked the beginning of the fascination with acronyms). These first computers were extremely large devices that employed vacuum tubes. ENIAC used almost 2,000 vacuum tubes and weighed about 30 tons. While certainly a marvel of ingenuity and creativity at the time, these early computers were not very reliable and were cumbersome and difficult to use.

The invention of the transistor brought the second generation of computers. The transistor greatly reduced their size, increased their speed, and with this increase in capacity, permitted greater ease of use as more sophisticated programming languages could be developed. The next important step, which occurred in the 1960s, was the development of integrated circuits. Integrated circuits permitted the placement of numerous electronic components, such as transistors, capacitors, and resistors on a small silicon wafer. This resulted in another dramatic decrease in size, increase in speed, and began to produce a very real savings in cost. This marked the third generation of computers.

Currently, the fourth generation of computers are becoming available. These computers are marked by VLSI or "very large-scale integration" and the presence of the ubiquitous computer chip. This large-scale integration has permitted sufficient numbers of components to be placed on a single silicon wafer so that the heart of the computer, the microprocessor, fits on a single chip. Again, great reduction in size has occurred, which, in turn, has triggered the personal computer revolution along with the development of the large, so-called super computers, such as the Cray-1. The power and ease of use of this current generation of computer is unparalleled, and these devices are making their way into the fabric of our society just as communication devices such as telephones, radios, and televisions have done. Certainly, exciting times are at hand as the fifth generation of computers are being developed. These computers will be devices with quite spectacular differences from the current generation, and the boundaries between human cognition and artificial intelligence will begin to blur as the structure and conceptualization of computer design changes.

However, for the present, the most significant impact of the computer revolution is the development of the personal computer. This device is relatively small, typically along the proportions of an electric typewriter, and its cost has been reduced to the point where a one or two thousand dollar investment is sufficient to purchase a quite powerful system. It is designed to be used by individuals rather than to be shared by large groups. Even the least sophisticated microcomputer dwarfs the capabilities of ENIAC.

As psychology has grown in sophistication as a science, so has our need grown for sophisticated tools to assist in both the research and applied aspects of the field. It is an exciting time for those who have become involved in this new technology. I find it difficult to imagine how it is possible to function without the use of these devices given the complexity and magnitude of many professional tasks. However, for those individuals who have not had the opportunity to become familiar with this technology, it often represents a complex topic that is intimidating enough to prevent easy exploration.

Thus, this book is intended to help attenuate some of the complexity and mystique of the interface between computer technology and psychology.

It is also intended to provide sufficient overview and basic information so that the reader will be able to delve into this marvelous technology easily. This guidebook is neither designed to teach hardware design nor computer programming, nor is it designed to function as a consumers' comparative guide to products. I hope, however, it will serve as a guide and stimulus to investigate computer utilization more fully and to help the reader determine if this marvelous generic tool is, in fact, appropriate and desirable for his or her specific professional activities.

CLINICAL UTILIZATION OF MICROCOMPUTER TECHNOLOGY

Chapter 1
Overview of Microcomputer Systems

CYBERPHOBIA

Cyberphobia appears to be a quite real phenomena and frequently manifests itself as an irrational refusal to become acquainted with and to utilize a computer or computer-related devices. It often reminds me of the pattern of behavior seen in young children who refuse to eat a particular food item and who in later years in retrospect, can't imagine why they avoided this item which now gives them such great pleasure. However, this fear of computers is not simply associated with novelty, as these individuals are often quite comfortable with other gadgets in their environment that purport to make some of life's tasks easier. I believe it is probably more related to perceived control than to any other variable. The computer is one of the rare tools we utilize that imposes a clear structure upon our interaction with it. Indeed, it is not uncommon to observe people talking to their computers. Depending upon the software, either software that is written and developed by the individual or software that is simply being used by the individual, the computer appears to take on certain personality characteristics. More precisely, the computer's behavior becomes somewhat predictable, and therefore it is frustrating when the computer does not behave predictably. Contrary to the continuing popular beliefs, computers do not make errors. It is really a non sequitur to propose such fault to a computer. Errors of the type typically reported would require judgment to take place and, of course, this is not the process. The "errors" that are observed are simply the result of incorrect information provided to the computer and thus, it perpetuated the incorrect information by incorporating it into its activities and products. Thus, this feeling of "personality," or somewhat predictable behavior comes into play when one begins to interact with the computer as if it had clear limitations. Such limitations are usually produced by the type of software being used. Thus, the computer is often characterized by terms such as "forgiving," meaning simply that it appears to compensate for user error, or "unfriendly" or "stupid" when it fails to permit a form of interaction that is not part of its current options. In other instances, the computer provides the illusion that it is "finicky" in that on different occasions it will appear to function properly and at other times appear not to function properly. The grand illusion to all of this is that there is actually minor variation in the user's behavior and this is imperfectly reflected back to the user through the interaction with the computer. This is the primary source of the supposed inconsistent characteristics that many individuals attribute to the computer.

I confess that I spend innumerable hours talking to my computer as if it could listen, and it is fascinating to self-monitor the type of interchange that takes place. Because the computer is interactive, the experience is much like carrying on a conversation with another person. I type certain commands into the computer and it responds. When it responds in a way that I had not anticipated, I type further commands. It again responds with a new variation and I continue with my requests. This proceeds in a give-and-take fashion and can produce a great deal of frustration because the computer is essentially acting as a mirror. That is, the errors, in fact or in programming logic, that I commit are immediately reflected back to me in all of their absurdity or illogic. Very much like a slot machine, the computer provides intermittent reinforcement. The thrill and feeling of achievement at having a program work properly is difficult to describe. Some have likened it to a game of chess in that it is a structure that involves moves and countermoves. However, this analogy is inadequate because there is less constraint upon the interaction between a person and the computer. Since the computer does only what it is programmed to do, at an intellectual level, although not at an emotional level, one's opponent is indeed oneself.

Thus, this period of exercising control and making the computer perform in a predictable fashion takes some time and has a clear, normal learning curve associated with it. There are aspects of this learning procedure that are similar to learning a foreign language (one must learn the computer language and syntax) and there are certainly unfortunate cultural "baggage" acquired through popular press, movies, and television that these devices are terribly intelligent and sensitive and that we as individuals often can do dire harm to them. I have met many individuals who quite literally believe that by pressing the wrong button, they can make the computer explode. Thus, in evaluating the use of a microcomputer as a professional tool, one must take into consideration not only personal usage, but also what demands, if any, will be placed upon other individuals to participate in this process. It would be wise to discuss any expectations and fears, if any, and to come to some mutually agreeable understandings.

However, given all the potential negatives and difficulties associated with becoming a viable computer user, the computer is one of the best toys ever invented. I use the word toy because it connotes an object or device to which the user must add some dimension of creativity and imagination and that can be both stimulating and enjoyable. Most toys in and of themselves are not terribly exciting or stimulating, rather it is what one does with toys and the structure it imposes on certain isolate interactions or social interactions that make them valuable. In like manner, the computer as a toy has the same effect and no doubt over the years, an important area of research will develop as to how computer interactions, from the video game to the true microcomputer as a generic tool, will influence the way in which children learn as well as how adults will function in society.

The term, *computer hacker*, is a common one, as is the rather unkind characterization of the computer nerd. What is interesting to recognize here is that in fact the computer is serving as a potent stimulus for interaction and as a unique device to maintain sustained interaction. It literally forces one to interact in a pattern quite atypical from the normal person-to-person interactions and demands clarity of communication that most of us, even the skilled clinician, are not used to and are unskilled at. However, as in many areas of fear and conflict, having an understanding of the factual information, engaging in some rational self-talk and a reasonable program of desensitization will typically result in a positive outcome so that one can greatly benefit from this powerful generic tool.

A RATIONAL APPROACH

It would be a mistake to obtain a microcomputer system simply because it is the current fad. As a tool it only has a function if there are particular tasks that require it. A good rule of thumb is to observe if one is confronted either with a series of repetitive, lengthy tasks that are easily quantifiable but take valuable time away from other activities, or tasks that are difficult to classify and quantify. Tasks that are repetitive and lengthy, such as the preparation of standard aspects of reports (e.g., descriptions of particular assessment devices), the preparation of monthly billing statements, the scoring of questionnaire information, the statistical analysis of data, and the collection of psychophysiological information are ideal for the microcomputer. To ascertain your needs and the desirability of a microcomputer system, a simple task analysis is appropriate. Make a list of the tasks and activities performed on a routine basis, the time spent in each of them, and a simple weighting as to whether these tasks are repetitive and essentially mechanical, or tasks that are too infrequent, complex, or poorly defined to be amenable to computer utilization. Then calculate the time savings that would accrue and compare it to the costs involved in acquiring a microcomputer system. Break each task listed as a potential candidate for computerization into sections. The first section should describe what information is available at the start of the task. The second section should describe what operations or manipulations must be performed on this information. The third section should describe the final format in which the information should be presented. Here is a simple example concerning client billing. Information necessary to prepare a statement might include:

1. first name
2. last name
3. address
4. telephone number
5. date of first contact
6. dates of sessions not yet paid for
7. the service performed in each session
8. the fee associated with each service

The process that would be involved would be to search all client records and to extract only those sessions that have not yet been paid, to recall the demographic information, and to present it in a columnar fashion with totals. Further, it may be desirable to present an aged accounting picture, that is, fees that are overdue by 30 days, 60 days, 90 days, and so on. For the final step, one would take either a standard billing statement or sketch out the exact statement that one would wish a client to receive along with perhaps one of a variety of dunning statements that would be related to the pattern of the previous payments.

Another example might be the creation of a data base to track polypharmacy among residents of a psychiatric facility as part of a long-term research project. In this case, one would require:

1. a coded subject identification number
2. information as to age, sex, diagnosis
3. date of admission
4. history of previous admissions
5. length of current stay
6. for each medication received, its name, dosage, and schedule of administration along with comments concerning rationale for administration
7. the presenting problem being addressed as well as notes concerning side effects and specific responses to the medication

In the second step, one would specify the type of analysis desired, such as comparison of individuals by diagnosis with both medication type and dosage, an analysis of most side effects, the most common combination of medications, or perhaps an analysis to select records based on the presence of certain a priori stated combinations of medications. In the third step, one would again sketch out a report format that would indicate specifically where certain information would be placed and how it would be summarized. One would also indicate if a variety of report formats were needed (e.g., by individual summed across each medication, or perhaps by diagnosis or age).

This task of outlining the specific requirements is typically not difficult if one is familiar with the process. However, for someone unfamiliar with the process, it can be an extremely difficult task and a salesperson is usually unable to help unless he has specific background in your area of expertise. However, given this three-part task analysis, the salesperson who is knowledgeable about computer hardware and software can easily take the information and help select an appropriate system. Essentially all that is required is to view this analysis as a series of different variables that will have certain relationships to one another. Whether those variables are MMPI subscores or the yearly high for a particular stock on the stock exchange is of minor importance. What is important is the data structure to be utilized, the type of storage required, the arithmetic manipulations, and the sorting capabilities as well as the capabilities to format this information into a meaningful report that is relatively jargon-free, and presented in plain English rather than in a coded form.

One value of this written analysis approach is that it can serve as the basis of a contract when a system is purchased. There are simply too many areas for ambiguity and misunderstanding that can result in receiving a microcomputer system that was "supposed to" perform all the desired functions, and that, in fact, performs few if any of the desired functions at an adequate level. However, by having some documentation one can eliminate such confusion and certainly hold the vendor accountable to ensure that the functions requested are provided.

As a provider of hardware and software, and also as a consumer, I've had a unique opportunity to view both sides. At times I am still amazed at the lack of correspondence between what appears to be a product's characteristics based on advertisements and its actual functioning. Oftentimes, although I believe I have made myself clear to a salesperson as to my requirements, there remain ambiguities and misunderstandings that are heightened when dealing with relatively expensive items. On the other hand, it is often terribly frustrating as a provider of both hardware and software to deal with demands by customers who simply assume that various products will perform in a certain fashion, who display no concern prior to or during the purchase, but who express great displeasure when they finally realize that their purchase was an error. Sometimes this error is based on understandable miscommunication, but often it is based on an individual's unwillingness to adequately study the problem and to gain some information about this complex endeavor. For example, I vividly remember a prosperous and well-educated individual who purchased a microcomputer system to track many inventory items and their specific utilization. This person became furious when he found that the information was not already contained within his microcomputer. That is, it had never occurred to him that he could only retrieve information that he had entered. When the enormity of the task of entering the thousands of items of inventory was apparent, he quickly understood that it would take him more time than he had available and would indeed have to hire additional staff to assist in the process. It is important to question one's assumptions about what a microcomputer system will do and certainly to be wary of salespersons who concentrate more on what their particular hardware and software can do for you than in questioning you about what your needs are and the specific parameters of those needs.

THE JARGON OF
THE TECHNOLOGY

It is often a humbling experience to delve into the microcomputer technology area and be confronted with its jargon. Indeed, it is also humorous to watch the interchange between a psychologist and a salesperson where one is using terms such as random access, CRT, pixel density, and megabytes of storage, while the other is using terms such as behavior analysis, MMPI, GSC, and *DSM III*. The jargon of the computer industry is not too difficult to decipher and the glossary at the end of the guidebook should help the neophyte. It is certainly appropriate consumer etiquette to ask for a translation of this jargon into colloquial English and to beware of the individual salesperson who is unable to do so. In like manner, however, it is important that the consumer translate professional jargon into colloquial English for the salesperson. It would be unusual to find a salesperson who is familiar with the particular needs of a psychologist.

Relative to the overall sales in the computer industry, sales to psychologists and other related professionals represent but a tiny fraction. To most salespersons, reference to the MMPI will conjure up images of some association with a federal agency such as the FBI. Thus there can be no real substitute for seeking out firms that specialize in the production of software and hardware for clinical purposes. Fortunately there are a growing number of such firms and they typically advertise in our journals, professional newspapers and newsletters. A partial list is contained in the reference sections of the guidebook and should help you find applications to meet your needs. However, as a general rule, the local computer retail store will provide the hardware at less expense than a firm that focuses specifically upon psychologists as their market. The primary reason for this lowered cost is a significant difference in the volume of sales for the respective firms. Thus one can often save significantly by doing some background research, going to various computer stores, purchasing hardware that is required and then seeking out and purchasing the relevant software. The only caveat to this process is that one should be certain that the particular software desired is in fact designed to be compatible with the specific microcomputer that has been chosen.

A very painful experience that occurs for the neophyte is that after the purchase of the rather expensive hardware, it is realized that, in fact, the microcomputer is prepared to do virtually nothing to assist in your professional activities. The microcomputer is certainly an extremely powerful and versatile tool. But it is also a unique tool in that it is only half of the required system. That is, while emphasis is placed on the hardware of the microcomputer system, less sensitivity has arisen about the need for, and the difficulties with, appropriate software. The microcomputer cannot be intelligent or versatile in the absence of sophisticated software. It is the software that makes the components interact appropriately and allows the user to perform a wide variety of useful functions.

To make matters even more complex, there is little standardization as to the particular functions that a given piece of software will perform even though its name implies certain specific functions. For example, there are literally scores of word processors available, as well as equal numbers of data bases, statistical programs, financial modeling programs, and so on. Each has its own unique characteristics and it is conceivable that for a given user, only a few programs of the scores available within a particular category would be appropriate for his needs. Indeed, the more specialized the activity, the more likely that this will be the result. Therefore, important questions must be asked during the decision process for acquiring a microcomputer and these questions must go beyond the simple generic statement that one "needs a word processor and data base." Such sensitivity to the complexity of the matter discriminates between the individual who has "an outmoded" computer, purchased many years ago that still performs exactly the functions that its owner requires, versus the individual who has just spent a great deal of money on state-of-the-art hardware and is at a loss to make productive use of the microcomputer system. Thus, although the hardware is an important component of the microcomputer system, it is not the most important. The most important component is the software one utilizes to make this generic tool function in a specific manner appropriate to one's needs.

BASIC CONCEPTS

Now we will assess the commitment of the faint of heart. This next section as well as chapters 2 and 3 will be a bit technical. The purpose is to lay a reasonable base of information about the basics of hardware and software operation. While this background is not mandatory and the reader could indeed skip to the applications chapters, a little exposure to the technology at this point will serve well in beginning the process of becoming a confident user rather than a reluctant bystander. The basic concepts are not very complex, but are simply somewhat foreign, and background in electronics is not needed.

The currently available microcomputers are technological wonders and have impressive capabilities. While they are indeed technologically sophisticated and their operating principles quite complex, there are but a few basic concepts that need to be mastered in order to use these devices productively. First, the heart of these devices is a large-scale integrated circuit package known as the CPU. This is the heart of the computer. It handles the most basic calculation and control functions. However, in and of itself, it is useless. It demands a host of circuitry known as the support logic. This support logic allows the CPU to access memory, produce video images, receive input from a keyboard or other device, and permits storage of information on a permanent basis to devices such as magnetic tape drives, floppy disk units, and hard disk units.

It is perhaps easiest to conceptualize this system as an interrelated network of modules with each module having semi-autonomous control over particular functions. For instance, when one is using the keyboard of the computer and typing in a command which is simultaneously seen on the video screen, a number of different processes are taking place. First, at the keyboard level, as each key is depressed, a switch is closed and a signal is transmitted to the circuitry of the keyboard interface. Each key stroke must be translated to a unique number which can then be further processed. Also the circuitry must ensure that if several keys are pressed quickly, almost simultaneously, it is able to decode the proper sequence and further, it must be able to detect if a key is being held down. On most keyboards, holding down a key indicates that the action should be repeated continuously at a high rate of speed, such as moving the cursor across the video screen. All of this requires a fair amount of sophisticated logic circuitry and results in a stream of information being sent to the central processing unit. This information is typically in a format known as ASCII. In this conventional format each symbol on the keyboard has a specific numerical value. For instance, a capital "A" has the value 65, a capital "B" 66, capital "C" 67, and so on. A small "a" has the value 97, small "b" 98, a small "c" 99, and so on. Thus, because of this system, it will become apparent why microcomputers tend to respond differently depending on whether information is typed in capital letters or small letters. As an example, when one types the command "RUN" into the computer to execute a program, the numerical information actually being received is different if the sequence is in capital letters or in lower-case letters. In using particular programs with certain computers, this problem is obviated as the software scans this incoming information and, if it is command information from the keyboard, quickly recalculates and converts the lower-case information into upper case by subtracting the constant 32.

Perhaps the most important general guideline to remember when first using computers is that they have a wide range of functions and abilities, but these functions are not always implemented for each computer and each application that you will be conducting. The computer can always perform more than it currently does, given proper modifications, to either the hardware or the software.

The next major section of the microcomputer is the video display. This is a cathode ray tube (CRT) similar to that in a television set, which is specifically designed to work at very high frequencies (which translates to high resolution). Many of the earlier microcomputers and a number of the current home-type microcomputers are designed to output their video signal to a home television set. One notices quickly, however, that the quality of the image is poor and there is little resemblance to that achieved on a computer monitor. This has to do with a characteristic known as bandwith, which is related to the internal frequency with which the monitor is operating. A video monitor is a necessity, not an option, for professional applications.

The most elementary information displayed to the video monitor is a representation of each of the symbols present on the keyboard. Thus, as a key is depressed on the keyboard, the above mentioned translation takes place. This information is passed to the CPU and simultaneously is fed to the circuitry that controls the video display. Here, a fairly complex circuit generates the proper synchronization signals for the video monitor and also utilizes an integrated circuit known as a character generator. This device takes the numerical information being received and translates it into the individual letters, numbers, and symbols on the keyboard through what is essentially a table stored in its own memory area. Each symbol, letter, or number is composed of a series of very small dots that can be seen on close examination of the monitor screen. These dots are known as pixels. In general, these pixels are arranged in a matrix of five across by eight down. Within this rectangle, each letter, number, and symbol can be constructed by turning on the appropriate pixel. Using this matrix to generate specific characters by changing the pattern of which pixels are on or off is analogous to electric billboards that use individual lights to form messages. Thus it is the character generator that specifies this pattern of on and off pixels within each matrix to form the letters and symbols that are being typed on the keyboard. The current standard is that there should be 80 such matrixes horizontally on the video monitor and 24 vertically. This results in what is referred to in the vernacular as "24 lines of 80 columns." This system approximates about ½ to ⅓ of a typical typewritten page. The video circuitry and character generator respond not only to the keyboard, but also to commands from the CPU to display information that the computer is generating.

A second type of display is known as a graphics display. In this modality the character generator is typically bypassed and each pixel is controlled individually. In this manner the apparent resolution of the screen is increased and one can produce displays such as graphs, schematics, and even crude pictures. Depending on the particular microcomputer utilized, the sophistication of the video generation section, and also the resolution of the video display monitor, extremely high-quality images can be displayed. This degree of resolution can vary extensively. For instance, for the standard Apple IIe computer, the resolution is 192 by 280, for the IBM PC basic computer, the resolution is 200 by 320, and for the Northstar Advantage computer it is 240 by 640. This range is extensive and the quality of the graphic images that can be produced vary significantly. This fact would be particularly important if one were interested in displaying cumulative records or standard frequency line graphs that encompassed many sessions of information. The higher the resolution available, the smoother the lines portrayed will be. If one is plotting relatively few points of information, this consideration is not important. However, if visual presentation of large quantities of information is a priority, this should be investigated carefully. Since we've determined that microcomputers can do more than is often apparent given changes in hardware and software, one can, for instance, modify the Apple IIe quite easily by expanding its memory capability and using a software program that generates 192 by 560 pixels of resolution. Thus, in comparing different microcomputers, one must be sensitive not only to standard features, but also to the options that are available.

As we go "deeper" into the microcomputer, we examine the random access memory that the central processor utilizes to perform many of the desired functions. This memory area is used to store the programs that are being utilized to form data arrays and to store individual characters when one is engaged in word processing or similar manipulation of text strings. Memory requirements vary greatly in the different microcomputers and many have an upper limit as to how much memory they can easily access directly. This is based upon the particular type of CPU being utilized. As an example, for an eight bit CPU such as the 6502 type which is used in the Apple computer, or the Z80 type which is used in a wide variety of microcomputers, the limit is 64K of memory which can be addressed. This is a function of the largest number that can be specified by the CPU. With one bit of information, one can specify only 0 and 1 as the numbers. With two bits of information one can specify up to the number 3. With three bits of information one can specify up to the number 7, with four bits up to the number 15, and so on. With eight bits this limit is the number 255. The CPUs mentioned are termed eight-bit processors and are eight bits "wide." The terminology is somewhat misleading as they actually have a 16-bit address bus for memory access. Sixteen bits permits specifying numbers up to 65,636. Unfortunately there is also a tendency to use the terms, *bit* and *byte*, interchangeably and inconsistently. The easiest way to view the relationship between the two is as a matrix:

	Bits								
	1	1	2	3	4	5	6	7	8
	2	1	2	3	4	5	6	7	8
Bytes	3	1	2	3	4	5	6	7	8
	4	1	2	3	4	5	6	7	8

Each byte is composed of 8 bits. Thus 64K of memory is a matrix of 64,000 locations, each with 8 bits. There are many variations such as 16-bit devices, in which case there would be 16 columns, but the important aspect is that it is a matrix, and each cell may have only the value of 0 or 1. The largest number able to be specified by an "8 bit" CPU (using its 16-bit address bus) is thus 65,636. Now, of course, if you have been following the mathematics here, you see an immediate discrepancy as it was said that the upper limit was 64K worth of information. However, it is an unfortunate truth in the computer industry that, to paraphrase the Queen in *Alice in Wonderland*, the meaning of the words and terms used in this industry vary as a function of perspective and implied understanding. Based on a history of conventions, approximations, and the normal process of jargon development within an area of expertise, the two numbers may be seen as essentially equivalent. That is, the difference between them is not seen as an important difference.

Thus, by sending out signals from the 16 "lines" of the CPU known as the memory address bus, the CPU can access individually each of these approximately 64,000 memory locations. Each location can be given a value, by assessing a 0 or 1 for each of the eight bits, and these patterns can then be translated into more easily understood information for the user. For instance, in a particular eight-bit segment of memory, the number 65 could be portrayed by the eight-bit sequence of 10000010. This, of course, corresponds to the capital letter "A." Thus by analyzing each of these eight-bit segments, this binary information can be translated to the numbers, letters, symbols that we see on the video screen and that we enter through the keyboard.

Related to random access memory are integrated circuits known as read only memory (ROM). These devices, as their name implies, permit only a one direction transfer of information. That is, information can be read from these devices, but new information may not be placed in them as is the case with random access memory. The purpose of ROM is multi-faceted and one example would be the character generator, where set patterns are required and can be accessed by the CPU without giving up precious RAM space. In some microcomputers the operating system of the computer, that is a series of integrated programs and instructions that allow the CPU to "talk" to the various devices that are connected to it, is stored in ROM. This permits this type of different memory space to be utilized while keeping free the RAM, which is used for primarily unique information, such as data that the user may enter. Interestingly, ROM devices are also known in some cases as "personality modules." That is, depending on the particular ROMs that are inserted, it changes the basic functions and capabilities of the microcomputer.

While ROM devices retain their basic information even after power to them is turned off, RAM devices do not. When power is turned off to RAM devices, all the information that had been stored is permanently lost. Thus, it is desirable to have storage devices that can take information from RAM and put it on media that are not volatile. When the microcomputer is used again at a future time, this information can be retrieved rapidly and placed back into random access memory. Therefore, the user can begin essentially at the point at which he had ended his previous session. Currently, the three most popular mass storage devices are magnetic tape, floppy diskettes, and hard disk units. These devices are highly related in that their basic operation consists of transferring information from RAM onto magnetically coated media. Magnetic tape is similar to an audio cassette tape unit, and the encoding system is almost identical. Floppy disks are circular magnetic media that rotate at high speed within a vinyl plastic jacket. These devices are analogous to phonograph records. The advantage to using disks lies in the ease with which information can be accessed. In order to find a particular segment on tape it is necessary to search linearly and sequentially through the tape, much as one would fast foreward on a cassette tape or video tape. This process can be tedious and lengthy. The diskette, however, rotates in a circular fashion and the device known as the "read/write head" moves across the surface of the media. Much as one can lift the needle on a phonograph, move it across the record, and select a particular track of music, one can do the same with the diskette. Thus, this device is often referred to as a random access storage device. Its advantage lies not only in the amount of information that can be stored easily, but also in the greatly increased speed with which particular pieces of information can be accessed in any particular order.

A relative of the floppy disk is the hard disk. This device is essentially the same as the floppy disk except that the media is on a rigid surface, spins at a much higher speed, and has a much higher density of storage on the media itself. Here again, there is an increment in both speed and amount of storage compared to the floppy disk, which, in turn, is better compared to magnetic tape. While hard disk units in the past were considered a luxury and were very expensive on microcomputers, the current rapid change in technology has been such that a hard disk unit is not only very common, but also a highly desirable device for the microcomputer.

Next in line of these "peripherals," or devices ancillary to the CPU, is a set of circuitry that allows information to be transferred from the microcomputer to a printer. This is often a confusing aspect of the microcomputer system. Reference is made to the printer interface, which is the assembly of electronic devices that communicate between the microcomputer and the printer. Unfortunately, specific reference is not made as to which of the multiple interfaces is being described. That is, within the microcomputer there are typically one or two of the current standard printer interfaces. The first and the oldest standard is known as parallel. This means that the microcomputer is transmitting eight data lines (again referring to eight bits) to the printer along with various other communication lines that provide transfer of information between the microcomputer and the printer concerning status, such as ready to send information, ready to receive information, indications that the printer may be out of paper, the ribbon may be empty, and so on. This is a high speed form of communication and involves relatively simple circuitry. This interface in the microcomputer is attached to the printer via cable. On the printer there is an analogous parallel interface which translates this information to the mechanism of the printer itself. Here also, one finds a character generator and the same matrix of dots used to form each individual character or symbol. In fact the most popular printers that use this type of mechanism are referred to as dot matrix printers. They will vary a great deal with respect to their resolution, just as video monitors do. Many dot matrix printers, similar to the video display screen, utilize a 5×8 dot matrix. However, others may use 10×12 dot matrixes or even up to 18×24 dot matrixes. Analogous to the video display monitor, the density of this matrix directly translates to the quality of the printed image that can be achieved.

A second type of interface in the microcomputer is known as a serial interface. This is somewhat more complex electronically and as the name implies, it transmits the information in a serial or sequential fashion, one bit at a time. Often this necessitates only providing as few as four wires between the computer and the printer. However, serial communication has many variations to it, the most important of which is speed. The microcomputer can control the rate at which information is transferred.

This rate is often referred to as BAUD rate and ranges typically from 100 BAUD to 9600 BAUD. Roughly, if one divides by 10, the result is the number of characters per second being transmitted. In an area in which the word "standard" often has varying meaning, the BAUD rate of 300, 1200, and 9600 are common standards. However, many printers are still designed as standard parallel devices. Therefore, if one installs a serial interface into the microcomputer, the odds are high that one must also install a serial interface in the printer. This allows for compatible transmission between microcomputer and printer interface, and then for translation of these signals to the mechanism of the printer in order to produce the desired output. In general, there is no particular advantage to either of these two systems of interface, and parallel interfacing is usually less expensive. However, a wider and wider array of devices that require serial interfaces for their operation are becoming available. Thus, it is important at the time of the purchase to specify the range of activities for which the microcomputer will be used and the particular peripherals that will be necessary. Usually, decisions made at that point are not irrevocable, but they can be costly in the future if translation has to be made from parallel to serial and vice versa.

A second type of printer is known generically as a daisy wheel printer. These are devices that operate much like typewriters. Instead of the individual characters being produced by a series of dots on the paper, they are "fully formed" by having the characters, which are molded onto a plastic or metal wheel, strike the ribbon which in turn strikes the paper. These produce what is termed "letter quality" printing or as some people refer to it, typewriter quality printing. Dot matrix printers are in general relatively inexpensive compared to the letter quality printers. The most important factor other than cost between the two is a speed by quality interaction. That is, letter quality printers produce excellent quality, but at very low speeds, typically in the range of 10 to 25 characters per second. In contrast it is not unusual for dot matrix printers to print in the 100 to 200 character per second range. There are some interesting new printers that combine relatively high speed with letter quality and conversely, high-quality dot matrix that do not compromise high speed. In both cases however, these devices tend to be expensive compared with their counterparts, and the user will find the choice of a printer perhaps one of the most difficult items for the microcomputer system. It is not unusual, and in many cases it is highly desirable to buy a basic high-speed dot matrix printer for producing drafts and internal documents, and a relatively slow-speed and inexpensive letter quality printer to produce the final drafts. However, the decision can only be made by an analysis of the user's particular application and the amount and quality of paperwork that will be generated.

The newest printing device and perhaps the most exciting one is the laser printer. These devices are essentially copying machines of the generic Xerox-type. In these devices, the information coming from the microcomputer is translated into individual characters and a low-power laser is used to transfer this information as symbols to the drum of the copier/ printer. Toner is then applied, paper fed through, and the image transferred from the drum to the paper. Thus, one can conceptualize this device as being the same as an office copier except that rather than placing an original into the device, the computer, through the character generator and then through the laser, is essentially drawing the information on the drum and then producing standard output. These devices operate at a high speed and produce excellent quality. Unfortunately their $3,000 to $7,000 price range makes these devices prohibitive for many users. However, in coming years, this technology will certainly advance and prices for the consumer will fall. If one is preparing to produce rather voluminous reports, or if there is a need to mix high quality text with high quality graphics, then the new generation of laser printers may be quite cost effective and can significantly improve efficiency of the transfer of information.

There are innumerable other peripheral devices that can be utilized with the microcomputer ranging from speech synthesis to touch sensitive video screens to x–y plotters to devices that control laboratory equipment. However, these are not what would be considered basic components of the microcomputer system and thus will not be covered in detail. Reference will be made to them in different sections of this guidebook.

Chapter 2
Software

Appropriate software is the most important part of the microcomputer system. It is a wise strategy to investigate software first and then choose the hardware based on the software requirements. Having a state-of-the-art, expensive, whiz-bang computer is of little use if the software needed for an important task runs only on a "lesser" computer. Hardware comparisons are relative and should always be made in the context of the application software.

OPERATING SYSTEMS

An operating system is the basic software "glue" that connects the various peripherals and functions of the computer system. It is the operating system that understands how to store and retrieve data to diskettes, how to engage the printer, and how to display information onto the monitor. As such, except for ambitious programmers, the operating system is, in the jargon of the industry, "transparent" to the user. This simply means that when using an application program, these various functions appear to take place automatically without the direct intervention of the user. Thus, they are transparent, or noninteractive with the user.

There are a wide variety of operating systems and in general, they should not be of great concern to you. Each manufacturer either has its own specific operating system or uses one of a few "standard" operating systems. Thus, the choice of operating systems is actually more a function of the specific hardware you have selected.

Apple Computer currently uses their DOS 3.3 and PRODOS operating systems. In fact, the letters DOS stand for Disk Operating System. An apparent standard for the IBM personal computer is the MS-DOS operating system. However, even within the same manufacturer there are different systems. For instance, Apple Computer's new Macintosh computer has a highly specialized operating system that bears little resemblance to any other currently available.

The important point here, however, is that as a user of the microcomputer system you will rarely need to concern yourself with the operating system. Some individuals will place great weight upon the operating system, stating, for instance, that CP/M is a preferred system because there are many thousands of programs available that are compatible with it. However, any statement about "thousands of programs available" is quite misleading. The typical professional user will, in fact, rarely use more than a dozen programs, and is interested in the specific application programs that are useful for certain professional activities. An exception is the poor soul who becomes addicted to the sophisticated games and entertainment software available, and these individuals usually experience a large increase in their software library. However, most games are self-contained and in essence, have their own operating system so that their use is simple and automatic from the point of the user.

The operating system is, however, an important component of the microcomputer system, as it must function in a sophisticated and flawless fashion. Therefore, one must be careful about "piecing together" unrelated hardware and should especially be wary of "bargains." A good example of this is hard disk storage units. It is certainly possible to find generic hard disk storage units with their own particular interfaces that are much less expensive than those provided by the microcomputer system's manufacturer. However, critical to the use of these devices is whether or not the operating system can control these devices and perform the appropriate functions. Be *very* sure that you will have full compatibility. This is certainly an area where the novice would be encouraged either not to enter or to have an experienced colleague or consultant participate in the selection process. What should be an easy-to-use and sophisticated system can often become a nightmare of components and operating system are nonstandard and need constant modification to perform their tasks.

LANGUAGES

Just as we have different languages for verbal communication, there are various languages for the computer system. Some of the most common are BASIC and PASCAL, and these permit relatively easy control of the computer. A software program is nothing more than an assemblage of specific commands that are written in a specific language. The commands are interpreted by these languages and translated into machine language, which is the primary binary language of the microprocessor. Interpreted languages thus always produce slower running programs than programs written in machine language because there is this process of interpretation and translation. Often a program will be developed with an interpreted language, as it is much easier for the programmer to utilize, and then, it in turn will be translated into machine language via another software program termed a *compiler*. A compiler works very much like an interpreted language in that it takes each command and translates it into machine language, but it also goes a step further and allows one to store this converted machine language program in its primary state. Thus, when such a program is executed, it runs many times faster than the original form that was developed in an interpretive language.

As with operating systems, the languages themselves will be of little interest to the majority of users. These languages are important only if you wish to develop your own software program. This type of activity is immensely enjoyable and presents an interesting intellectual challenge. It is both an incredibly frustrating and rewarding experience to attempt to take a complex system of hardware and to control it through these software commands. As mentioned earlier, it is a completely logical system and thus, quickly becomes almost an alter ego with whom one does battle.

There are certainly many skilled computer users who have no programming background and who do not engage in programming. Rather they have purchased specific application packages that they have learned very well and can effectively use them as powerful tools. If a goal is to perform one's own programming, this should be viewed as a serious avocation, one that will consume a great deal of time and effort. It would be wise, if this is a goal, to participate in some seminars or courses on programming. Programming is not difficult to learn, it is simply analogous to learning a foreign language. However, different individuals demonstrate different proficiencies in learning languages and this is certainly the case with programming. One must learn the individual vocabulary of programming, that is, the particular commands and then their syntax, that is, how the commands are used in conjunction with one another. There is yet a third level however, and there is no clear analogy for it. Perhaps the closest is the differentiation we make when referring to someone who has difficulty in verbal expression versus someone we term as eloquent. Both are using the same language, but to very different levels of impact. The same is true for programming. It is this third level, creating the algorithm for the solution of a problem and creating the structure of the software program, that takes great skill and goes beyond the simple knowledge of the commands that are available. It is an enjoyable activity and one that can certainly result in great productivity, but it is nevertheless a process that requires patience, time, and energy and for the average person, may simply not be cost-effective, given the demands of other professional activities.

AUTHORING SYSTEMS

An extension of programming languages are authoring systems. These are essentially software programs that operate at a still higher level and that permit an individual to create software programs with a far smaller set of commands. The authoring system, in essence, generates the series of commands and structure that would be used in the typical language. A good example of such an authoring language is Pilot. This is a program specifically designed to allow teachers to construct lessons and examinations. Activities that would be very difficult and time consuming to program in a language like BASIC or PASCAL are very easy in an authoring system because the specific routines and procedures to perform certain functions have been completed and are part of the authoring system. What is important here however, is that these are not generic systems as is a language; the authoring systems are designed for a specific purpose and thus have clear constraints on their usage.

As an example, Pilot allows one to create lessons that are presented at a certain pace, to time the speed of response, to easily put questions into multiple-choice or fill-in-the-blank format, and to allow a search for a particular response in order to find key words that can ascertain whether the response was correct or incorrect. Pilot also permits easy formatting of test results and thus can be extremely useful for a nonprogrammer in creating computer-assisted instruction programs.

The user must be careful to precisely define what functions are required for the particular CAI project and to match these expectations with the actual functions available in a system like Pilot. Again, because it is a closed system, one does not have the programming freedom found in a programming language but is using a restricted menu of predetermined commands and functions. On the positive side, using such authoring systems is often a good entree into computer programming because there is a preexisting structure and the number of commands and complexity of the syntax is limited.

GENERIC PROGRAMS

Proceeding along this continuum, generic programs are designed to perform a specific function but have latitude within that function. The best example of this type of program is word processors. These programs permit one to enter text much as one would using a typewriter and to manipulate that text by "cutting and pasting" and moving things around. The program is generic in that the content is quite irrelevant, but the format is the focus. Another example of a generic program would be a spreadsheet. This type of software constructs an elaborate grid or matrix on the computer screen and permits one to enter descriptors, numbers, and formula into the various cells of the matrix and also permits one to interrelate these cells. It is often used for financial modeling and for budget preparation. Its power is that a change in any one cell will simultaneously produce a proportional change in other cells that are linked through a particular formula. Thus, if one was constructing a budget, one set of columns might contain an individual's base salary, the second column medical benefits, the third federal withholding, the fourth and other columns other benefits. These columns can be related to one another as a function of percentage of base salary. The final column might be the total, thus allowing one to look not only at the effect of a raise upon the base salary, but also at the total for which the agency would be responsible. A spreadsheet is the equivalent of a large sheet of paper with many columns and a very fast calculator. It can result in great time savings if properly utilized.

Generic programs can have positive impact upon productivity, as they neatly delineate certain types of activities and enhance efficiency in conducting these activities. However, even though these are generic programs, one will typically find various brands of generic programs within an activity. Here again it is important to assess the particular parameters and constraints of each different program and to ensure that they are compatible with the task that must be performed.

SPECIALIZED PROGRAMS

This type of program is perhaps most frequently found in the professional software library. It is a program designed to perform a particular task that is somewhat unique and usually specific to a profession. An example of this type program would be software to analyze the MMPI or a program that performs sophisticated data analysis of group design experiments. Such programs are usually authored by, or at least designed by, individuals with a primary background in the specific area of application and a secondary background in computer programming. Programs such as these can be extremely powerful and very useful. However, great caution must be observed in order to ascertain the credentials and skills of the software producers, as the task is no longer formatting words in a nice way on a sheet of paper or performing calculations. Rather, software of this specialized type often is being used to perform evaluations that, in turn, are utilized. Thus, not only is accuracy an important component, but also it is important to understand the manner in which the software was designed so that certain conclusions can be produced. This is an important topic that will be discussed more fully in chapter 14.

CUSTOMIZED PROGRAMS

In general, on this continuum of software, the customized program is the most useful and also the most expensive. In this case, a person can either write the software or hire a programmer to produce the actual software. The advantage of customized programs is that because the user is the designer, they will perform exactly as desired and thus, will be optimally efficient. Programs can be designed to both request and present information in a manner that takes into account any particular preferences or idiosyncrasies of the user. Also, the user is completely aware of the intricacies of the program and how it performs its functions. Thus, in performing specialized clinical or research activities this type of customized program would be the software of choice, although it would be an expensive option.

Chapter 3
Microcomputer Hardware

BASIC COMPONENTS

Specific applications will determine the final configuration of a microcomputer system. However, there are certain components that should be present in any microcomputer system. The first component is the microcomputer itself. This is typically a metal or plastic enclosure that contains the following basic components: a motherboard on which is located the CPU, ROMs, the video circuitry components, and other circuitry to connect to various peripheral devices. The enclosure also contains the power supply and connectors to permit access to the bus structure of the microcomputer. In the past, general terms such as "S-100 type," were used to describe the design approach used in certain microcomputers. This phrase simply referred to the internal connectors in the housing that had 100 contacts on the connectors, 50 on each side. This type of structure permitted other circuit cards to be inserted into the machine to add extra memory, disk drive controllers, video graphics options, and so on. More recently there has been a move toward an "all-in-one" motherboard, which is one large, main circuit board on which these options are built. Both types of designs are on the market today, and it is important to specifically ask what the relative costs and expansion capabilities of the machine are. It is important to remember that one is buying, in a sense, a host device into which many other devices will be linked. Somewhat related to the bus structure of the microcomputer and usually directly related to its speed of operation is the particular CPU that is utilized. The microprocessor is often referenced by a specific alphanumeric designation. In the Apple II line of computers, the 6502 microprocessor is used while in the relatively newer Macintosh, the 68000 microprocessor is utilized. The first, that is the 6502, is an 8-bit microprocessor while the latter is a 32-bit microprocessor. The IBM personal computer, released several years ago, uses a 8088 microprocessor which is a 16-bit CPU. Most of the desk top microcomputers over the past several years that use the CP/M operating system employ

FIGURE 3.1. An example of an early S-100 bus microcomputer. The raised circuit board has the characteristic 50 gold-plated contacts in its base.

an 8-bit microprocessor known as a Z80. All these devices represent an evolution of the technology of producing smaller and more powerful microprocessors. In many ways, it is not unlike reference to a '57 Chevy or a '68 Thunderbird. We recognize that such references are to generic types of transportation, although at the same time they specify a model of automobile that has distinguishing characteristics. The important point, however, is whether or not these characteristics are functionally discriminable to the user. While the technical specifications are indeed different and these various CPUs operate at different speeds, have different instruction sets, and can address more or less memory, the bottom line of evaluation is whether or not for the applications that you choose to utilize, will there be any noticeable difference. In many respects it is not unlike selecting stereo components that can record and reproduce sounds beyond the range of human hearing. While one can marvel at and appreciate such technology, it does little to enhance the listening pleasure of the average person. The same is true with respect to computer hardware. "Faster and more powerful" are relative terms that may or may not be significant for the typical user. Thus, it is important to remember that one is evaluating the performance of a system of components and should not be unduly swayed by the technical characteristics of any one component.

FIGURE 3.2. An example of a sophisticated motherboard approach, where the majority of the circuitry needed is on the motherboard itself. Optional circuit boards are installed in the small sockets to the rear of the motherboard.

MEMORY AND STORAGE

I can readily remember using microcomputers in which 2K of memory was considered a great deal. There seems to have been an amazing almost multiplicative rise in the amount of memory considered appropriate and necessary in microcomputers. A few years ago, 48K of memory was considered the norm and more than adequate. More recently in the CP/M based operating system machines, 64K was typically required. Now 128K and 256K are quite common with many machines utilizing .5 M and 1 M of memory. The reasons for this change are not primarily technological. They reflect not so much increasing sophistication of our devices, but rather the increasing sophistication of our software. The "user friendly" software that is now so highly desirable has a high cost associated with it with respect to memory requirements. As a general rule of thumb, one should look for a microcomputer with a memory capacity in the range of 128K to 512K. This should be more than adequate for most applications and in fact, for applications limited to word processing and simple record keeping 64K is quite sufficient.

With respect to data storage devices, the norm is clearly the floppy disk and the hard disk. I shall not cover the options available with respect to magnetic tape, as it is not appropriate for the typical user. The range of cost and storage capacity of floppy disks is quite extensive. There are at present three standard sizes: the 3½-inch disk, the 5¼-inch disk and the 8-inch disk. One finds a range of storage from anywhere between 100K and 200K per diskette to 1 M and beyond. However, beyond the cold figures of storage limit, it is important to realize that although the diskettes may be physically similar across machines, in general, these media are not transferable. That is, a diskette which has programs for the Apple computer cannot be read directly by an IBM computer. Even if programs are written in the same language, they cannot necessarily be transferred via the medium of the diskette between machines. It is true that there are certain hardware adaptations to allow such transfers, but they are often expensive and are not useful for the typical user.

Hard disk drives are in many ways similar to the floppy disk drives except that the magnetic material is sealed into the hard disk drive and may not be removed. These units are several times more expensive than the floppy disk drive unit, but they will typically store more than 20 times the amount of information. Currently, one finds a wide variety of hard disk units that store 5, 10, 15, 30, and more megabytes of information. At present, there are hard disk drives being manufactured that have removable disks that will further extend the utility of these devices.

For a typical microcomputer system, two floppy disk drives are useful. This permits not only the easy copying of diskettes to provide archival or "back up copies" should something happen to the working copies, but it also permits one to have various software programs located on one disk while the data associated with the programs are located on the second. This arrangement can be convenient in an office or research environment in which many different programs are being utilized. Given the current relatively low price of hard disk drives compared to those in previous years, it is also a recommended component of the microcomputer system. While it can be added at any time to your system, I would urge consideration of it from the beginning unless one is on a very tight budget. The hard disk provides an ease of operation and access to various program information that has very positive effects on the general utility of the microcomputer. Especially if one is contemplating using large data bases, then a hard disk unit is very desirable indeed.

There is one drawback, however, which must be considered. The tolerances in hard disk units are very small and thus, one typically speaks of not *if* the hard disk unit should fail, but *when* it will fail. Such failures usually result in a partial loss of stored data due to the rather colorful reference of hard disks "crashing." This description is not too melodramatic, because the read/write head of the hard disk traverses the surfaces of the disk at extremely high speeds. When a mechanical failure occurs, and the head descends upon the disk in incorrect sequence or at an inopportune time, the result is indeed much like a crash. Fortunately, there is a simple method of making a copy of the contents of the hard disk that is analogous to making copies of a floppy disk. The only difficulty is that the process is greatly expanded. That is, the hard disk unit may contain the equivalent information of 30 to 50 floppy disks. Thus, to back up the hard disks, one has to insert sequentially from 30 to 50 floppy disks and have portions of the hard disk copied onto each of these in a specific sequence. While this task is not difficult, it can become annoying and time consuming. Depending on one's evaluation of the probability of failure of the hard disk, one gets into an interesting pattern of making these back-ups. When I first received my hard disk unit, I made back-ups very frequently. However, as the probability of failure appeared to approach zero, the probability of my engaging in back-up behavior also began to reach zero. Given the high usage of my hard disk unit, it would be recommended to back it up at least twice a month. However, I must confess that I have not performed this task for more than a year, a fact that brings tears to the eyes of our computer hardware consultant. I often think the task of general "maintenance" is best delegated to someone in the office with lesser knowledge of the system who could incorporate these activities routinely into their other normal office or assistant activities and thus, "playing the odds" would be eliminated. For the truly compulsive owner this type of arrangement is, of course, unnecessary. Also, for the more affluent individual, alternatives exist. Devices known as tape back-ups or tape streamers may be installed with hard disks to provide back-up onto magnetic tape. This is a very fast and simple procedure that virtually eliminates the inconvenience of back-up to floppy diskettes. Such systems are a necessity with the high-capacity hard disks that store over 50 megabytes.

KEYBOARDS AND
VIDEO DISPLAYS

Many microcomputer systems have integral video displays and keyboards, thus producing an all-in-one or desk-top unit. Other types allow complete selection of interchangeable video displays and keyboards, while still others offer either attached or nonattached keyboards (that is a keyboard that is connected to the microcomputer via either a cable or infrared signals). Video displays span a wide range of sizes and colors, from the monochrome that have either a white, green, or amber phosphor, to color video displays that can produce much of the color spectrum. Video displays also span a range of resolution (i.e., the clarity with which individual characters or symbols are presented on the screen). The same general range appears for keyboards in that there are different physical keyboard layouts and often there can be significantly different tactile cues associated with various models, just as there are with common typewriters. For the video display and the keyboard components in particular, it is very wise to spend some time before purchasing and actually utilizing these devices in order to ascertain your personal reaction to the resolution and quality of the screen and the feel of the keyboard. If one were purchasing a microcomputer system for use primarily by office staff or research assistants, then I would strongly advise engaging the participation of these individuals, because quite often strong individual preferences appear along the dimensions described.

PRINTERS

Printers span an almost unwieldy range of choices. There are two basic types of printer: the dot matrix printer and the daisy wheel or letter-quality printer. As mentioned previously, these two types differ primarily along the dimensions of speed and quality. The dot matrix printers tend to be relatively fast, in the range of 100 to 200 characters per second and, with appropriate hardware and software, are able to reproduce exactly what appears on the video screen. This is advantageous when one is doing analyses that result in graphs or when constructing specialized visual stimuli. The versatility of the dot matrix printer is high and I recommend it without reservation as a necessary component of any microcomputer system. There are many different brands of these dot matrix printers and they cost from $200 to $300 for simple basic functions to $1,500 to $2,000 for printers that are high-speed, print in several colors, and offer great flexibility in the alteration of the character sets employed. In general, the dot matrix printers in the $250–$500 range are adequate for most purposes and one should be very cautious if requested to spend more than this amount.

Although it is almost a universal truth that any printer can be connected to any computer, it is important to realize that there are some basic factors that must be taken into consideration. As mentioned previously, the two communication standards are serial and parallel, and an electronic interface must be positioned between the printer and the computer. This interface acts as a referee between the two devices to direct both speed of communication and priority of communication. Each interface has various characteristics and abilities, but they are not necessarily interchangeable. Therefore, prior to purchasing, be sure that the interface for the printer chosen can indeed perform the full range of operations that you require. This is particularly true when evaluating the interface's ability to transfer graphic images from the video screen to the printer.

A second factor relevant to dot matrix printers is the type of paperfeed. Commonly, pin-feed is utilized in which small pins attached to a drive mechanism on the printer pull computer paper through the printer mechanism. The type of paper used has holes on the left and right margins with perforations next to these holes so they can be removed after printing. In the past, the quality of this paper was limited. Currently, it is easy to obtain paper at relatively low cost in a variety of weights, colors, and textures. Further, one can have one's own letterhead printed onto continuous feed paper and have the left and right margins perforated more finely than in the past. Therefore, when the pin-feed holes are removed, the paper is almost indistinguishable from typical letterhead. The pins on the printer are also movable so they may be readjusted to accept continuous form labels for printing mailing lists, postcards, or index cards. There are some occasions, however, on which it may be desirable to use single sheets of specialized paper (e.g., to produce ditto masters). Here, it is important to have a dot matrix printer that has "friction feed," much like a typewriter. On some dot matrix printers this is standard, while on others it is optional. Again, it is important to clearly understand the capabilities of the printer prior to making a purchase and to ensure that the characteristics that you find desirable are indeed present.

The second type of printer, the daisy wheel printer, produces a print quality very similar to typewriter quality. Printers of this type are often used for important correspondence and formal reports or manuscripts. While this type of printer excels at print quality, it has some drawbacks. First, it is not designed to produce graphic displays and therefore is limited only to typical text processing activities. The second major drawback is its slow speed. In the under $1,000 price range, these printers typically perform in the 10 to 20 characters per second range, which is significantly slower than the dot matrix printers. It is possible to obtain relatively higher speeds in the 50 to 60 character per second range, but these printers often cost $2,000 or more.

For most applications, I believe it is wise to choose a dot matrix printer and then consider adding a letter quality printer if there are certain tasks that demand this high quality output. The dot matrix type output is now becoming accepted, and it is no longer unusual to see clinical reports, manuscripts, and correspondence that utilize a dot matrix printer. Although at first blush it might seem extravagant, in most cases, it is less expensive and more versatile to obtain a moderate-cost dot matrix printer and a slow but inexpensive letter-quality printer so that one can produce the majority of output, especially drafts, at the greater speed, on the dot matrix printer and only the final copies and those few documents that demand letter quality on the daisy wheel printer. This combination will result in high efficiency and greater flexibility than purchasing even one of the relatively higher-speed, expensive daisy wheel printers.

ADDITIONAL PERIPHERALS

There appears to be an almost unlimited array of peripherals that can be used with a microcomputer. These include X-Y plotters that permit very high resolution drawings, such as graphs and diagrams that are suitable for use in journal articles. Also included are various input and output circuits that fully emulate the relay rack and solid state control devices in experimental laboratories, and they also emulate the analog equipment needed for biofeedback. Alternative forms of input to the computer exist such as joy sticks, touch sensitive keyboards and CRTs, temperature sensing devices, optical card readers, and voice recognition devices.

It is doubtful that any one user would want to acquire all of these peripherals. However, the point here is that it is important to ascertain the range of peripherals available for the particular microcomputer system you are investigating and their costs. It is often feared that a given system may soon become obsolete due to the rapid development pace of the microcomputer industry. This is a somewhat irrational fear because although other newer and more "powerful" microcomputers may be developed, the most important factor is whether or not the device you have chosen will maintain its flexibility and ease of use for your particular applications. Ensuring that a wide range of peripherals are available will greatly attenuate this concern of obsolescence.

MAINTENANCE

Given that the microcomputer system is a complex and integrated device, it is reasonable to be concerned about maintenance. The most vulnerable part of the system is not the computer itself, but the mechanical peripherals, which include the disk drive and the printer. These two devices will have the highest probability of failure, because they are mechanical and can simply wear out or become out of alignment or calibration. There are some simple steps that can be performed on a monthly basis to reduce the probability of failure or difficulty. These are included in the manufacturer's instructions: for the disk drive, simple cleaning can be performed in a few minutes, for the printer, instructions are for lubricating and keeping the unit clean and free from the dust and residue associated with the printing process. Common sense precautions, such as placing dust covers on all equipment, not permitting smoking near the machines, and keeping the environment generally clean are usually more than sufficient to ensure the continued operation of the equipment. In settings where power fluctuations may occur, it is a wise precaution to obtain a device known as a surge protector or spike protector. This fits between the electrical wall outlet and the power supply to the computer. In general, these devices are less than $50 and prevent fluctuations in power, especially surges that exceed the recommended nominal level, from reaching the computer power supply. While certainly not a necessity, this is a relatively low-cost device in proportion to the cost of your microcomputer system and an investment well worth making.

Maintenance contracts are available from most retail dealers or manufacturers. However, I would urge caution in evaluating these contracts. Given the typical fear the novice has that something will go wrong, he falls easy prey to maintenance contracts that are not cost effective. Part of this association comes from the high maintenance cost of large, mainframe computers that are in quite a different category. I have many microcomputer devices that are used in my clinical and research activities, and I have never regretted not placing them on a maintenance contract. I have found them to be extremely reliable, and the occasional repair cost is less than the cost of placing all of the systems on a maintenance contract. However, if one does achieve some peace of mind by having a maintenance contract, then an interesting index of the manufacturer's or retailer's confidence in the hardware would be a comparison of maintenance costs. In general, I find it a good rule of thumb that the lower the maintenance cost for a given microcomputer system, the higher the reliability of that system. However, whether or not one obtains a formal maintenance contract, it is important to become familiar with the operation of the various hardware components and the advised routine maintenance. It is a fascinating process to observe the speed with which one becomes quite dependent on these devices once they are incorporated into daily activities and it is quite painful indeed when they cease to function properly. As with any complex device, attention to the details of preventative maintenance will prove quite beneficial.

Chapter 4
Telecommunications

OVERVIEW

A growing use of microcomputers is to access information contained in other remote computers, which are computers separated by substantial distances. This is not a difficult procedure and is similar to the process that takes place when transferring information from a computer to a printer. Since the two computers cannot be connected physically, a device known as a modem is utilized. The computer transmits information via a serial interface to the modem, which translates the digital information into tones, which in turn, can be transmitted over standard telephone lines. The receiving computer must also have a modem attached and it functions in a reverse manner, translating the tones received over the telephone line into digital information, which is in turn, transferred to the receiving computer via a serial interface. However, a modem can perform both functions, that of receiving and transmitting information, so that two-way communication is possible.

While conceptually quite simple, the actual hardware and software is rather complex and tends to be a stumbling block for the novice. The primary reason is that there is a great deal of ''handshaking'' in logic taking place. Each computer must know when its counterpart is attempting to send and receive data and when its counterpart is busy processing data and therefore cannot participate in an interchange. Appropriate software must also be used that will translate the incoming information into a mutually compatible format and will allow each computer to still function independently, although cooperatively. The selection of software is very important as it can range from simply allowing your computer to serve as an auxillary keyboard and CRT to the ''host'' computer, to allowing your computer to dial automatically and connect to a remote computer at pre-programmed times of day and interrogate that computer, retrieve specific information, and store this information on the disk drive of your computer. Thus, one can invest as little as $150 on hardware and software for tele-

31

communications or as much as $500–$600 depending upon the specific purposes for which the computer will be utilized.

MAINFRAME COMMUNICATION

Most recent survivors of graduate school are quite familiar with the utilization of large, mainframe computers. In general, they tend not to be too user-friendly nor convenient. The functions that are available at the terminals in the typical university center are also readily available via telecommunications. For these specific uses, the microcomputer is often configured to emulate a "dumb terminal", so that only the CRT and keyboard appear functional. This means that the more advanced functions of the microcomputer are not being utilized, such as disk access, using specific application programs, or using your own programs. Rather, one is simply attaching to the main computer facility and utilizing the software features available through the mainframe computer.

This type of application typically represents a convenience rather than a unique application. One could certainly go to the university computer

FIGURE 4.1. A typical telecommunications system. The computer is connected to the modem (the small box under the telephone) and can display information on the screen, the printer, or save it onto a diskette.

center to use the mainframe computer. However, anyone who has spent significant amounts of time waiting in line to use a terminal or traveling across town or across campus only to find that the computer system is "down" knows that the convenience of having such a remote terminal in one's office or home is not insignificant.

INFORMATION SERVICES

Utilizing the same basic principles of connection discussed in the previous example, there is a very different class of mainframe computer services that one can access. These are typically referred to as information services or data-base services. These services are all similar in that they are comprised of several dozen different individual and specific data bases. For example, one can access data bases such as Psych Info (a data base of psychological publications maintained by the American Psychological Association), Dow Jones, airline reservations, Index Medicus (an index of medical literature), UPI and Reuters, NOAA weather reports, and so on. The wealth of information available is quite literally staggering. The ability to tie in to such services through the microcomputer allows speed and diversity of search for information that would put most libraries to shame.

To access these data bases, one subscribes to a long distance telephone service that provides reduced rates and then one also subscribes to the data-base service itself. Once connected to the service, one chooses which particular data base is to be accessed. Then, commands are entered that specify the subject and the particular parameters of interest, such as published reports on "biofeedback with adult females focusing on lowering blood pressure published since 1980." The literature base is then searched and usually in only a few seconds the references that meet the selected criteria are identified and may be printed on the computer screen. In like manner, these services allow one to request printed copies that are typically mailed within 24 hours of the request.

My first experience with this system made a lasting impact. In preparation for a review paper on self-injurious behavior, I wished to conduct an exhaustive literature search. While many individuals are familiar with the typical university library computer searches and the reams of paper that they produce, this was a unique experience for me. Sitting at the terminal connected to the service, I transmitted basic identifying information about the topic. Within less than 15 seconds, almost 40,000 articles in the psychological and medical data base had been searched. Of this, several thousand were identified as a positive match. At this point, a sample of individual articles were inspected and the search further refined (I indicated that references to suicide should be deleted. The size of the pool of references was thereby reduced). This process was continued in an interactive fashion—I made changes in the selection criteria, saw the results as they affected the types of articles being selected, and either added new selection criteria or deleted current ones. After about 15 minutes I had identified several hundred references and they arrived shortly thereafter in the mail with full citation and abstract. It was the most precise search I had ever had performed and clearly indicated that the traditional manner in which information is accessed in libraries for professional purposes will not be very long-lived. It is difficult to describe the impact, whether it be in research, administrative, or clinical activities. Quite literally from one's desk, it is possible to search tens of thousands of publications to determine if specific information exists and precisely where it exists.

A commonly heard lament is the difficulty of "keeping up with the literature." I can highly recommend this type of remote data-base approach and I believe it will clearly change some of the standards by which we currently judge the scope and breadth of review articles. Unfortunately, I must also balance this enthusiasm with an important caution, that these data bases are not user-friendly and can be difficult to interact with. The skill of the user will determine the accuracy of the search and its utility. Even though these services provide comprehensive user's manuals, I strongly recommend that one attend the seminars offered by these various services. Seminars provide hands-on experience and usually last one or two days. Given this training, one should have no qualms about effectively utilizing these services. Also, several new software programs have appeared which run on microcomputer and serve to ease the interchange with the remote data base by helping the user formulate the search and then transmitting the appropriate information to the data-base service. Programs of this type will greatly assist the user in performing accurate and efficient searches. However, in the absence of such specific training or software assistance, accessing these various services can become either a frustrating and wasteful experience (as one is charged for the time connected to the service), or it can simply become rather sophisticated entertainment if used to interrogate the stock market, UPI, or to find out the current top ten grossing movies.

ELECTRONIC BULLETIN BOARDS

One of the most fascinating developments in recent years, both from sociological perspective as well as from a computer user's perspective, is the development of electronic bulletin boards. Much as the name implies, one uses a modem to tie into a host computer. The host computer runs sophisticated software that serves to post messages in a variety of categories and permits users to leave messages for one another. This type of service is often referred to as electronic mail. There has been an explosion of such bulletin boards and, in fact, there are now bulletin boards that are simply lists of bulletin boards. They range from small systems devoted to local computer hobbyists, to systems that serve purposes similar to the CB craze of a number of years ago, to systems that are used to solicit explicit sexual contact, to sophisticated resources for professionals. Many of these electronic bulletin boards, and there are literally hundreds, are fascinating to play with but are of little value to the professional. I have found that they can be quite addictive as one essentially "browses" through the various categories listed and then reads the messages and announcements that are available. However, if one is operating a typical modem which transmits approximately 30 characters per second, one's telephone bill can add up rapidly although this is a pleasant reading speed. Thus, it can be a rather high-priced form of entertainment, although I must add that it is enjoyable.

Recently, a bulletin board system explicitly for psychologists has been initiated by Academic Applications in San Antonio, Texas. This bulletin board system is a very important development and contains a wealth of information. There are over a dozen different categories ranging from issues discussing hardware, software, journals, requests for clinical information, and so on. I have spent many an hour using this system and have always found useful, timely information. In many ways it is similar to attending a conference except that people are not face to face. One can raise general questions and leave them on the public bulletin board, or pose specific queries to individuals who have left previous messages. This type of information transfer process has some unique advantages compared to the more traditional format. Certainly one could raise the question, why not simply write a letter to the person with whom you wish to communicate as it does not involve computer hardware or telephone time? Or, for that matter, why not simply telephone the person directly and speak over the phone? For many types of communication, this is in fact, an appropriate criticism. On the other hand, when one is seeking to obtain information from a group of people sharing similar interests, the bulletin board can be highly effective. For instance, if one wishes to know what particular data-base software is appropriate for a certain application, a message on the bulletin board will ensure that many individuals—the majority of which you probably do not know personally and therefore could not contact by letter—will see this information and will be able to respond. This is analogous to discussion hours at a convention, which can often be extremely productive, but also are costly and infrequent. As the electronic bulletin board system by Academic Applications continues to grow, I believe it will be a multifaceted influence and a resource that many will use.

Chapter 5
Administrative Uses

Whether in academic, research, or clinical service settings, administrative tasks are often time consuming and tedious. They are rarely difficult in and of themselves, but involve a great deal of time and energy, and are often frustrating because the tasks require utilizing the same basic information in several different formats. Certainly word processing is a useful function and will be discussed in the next chapter. There are other aspects, however, to administrative tasks that can produce substantial increases in efficiency and make the administrative burden more tolerable.

BILLING

The preparation of statements for clients and the preparation of insurance forms is a tedious and time-consuming task that often results in errors. One approach to this task is to use a data base to construct a set of procedures to manage this information (see chapter 7). However, for the typical user, this is not an efficient method of approaching the problem. It is far more efficient to purchase a specialized software program written especially for the purpose of billing for psychological services. Most such programs are, in fact, written by psychologists or psychiatrists and are quite extensive in their capabilities. Billing systems are complex enough that they must draw upon expertise not only in the area of clinical practice and accounting, but also on rather sophisticated computer programming skills. Most developers have spent several years preparing these programs and the typical user probably would not find this activity attractive or even feasible. In general, such programs are moderately expensive (i.e., in the $300 to $500 price range). This is a small investment when one considers the program's capabilities, and recently software in the under $100 price range has appeared.

The psychologist's type of practice, whether individual or group, full-time or part-time, often determines the particular packages that one would investigate. The major, important characteristics of these programs are the abilities:

1. to construct a basic client demographic and treatment history file,
2. to specify services and their related costs to the client,
3. to prepare monthly statements and keep track of payment history,
4. to prepare specific insurance forms.

Such programs must be evaluated not only on their ability to meet these particular functions, but also on the ease of their use and, perhaps most importantly, on the degree of assistance provided by the vendor. Although not a requirement, it is certainly a good sign when either an 800 number telephone line or other telephone number is available for consultation and questions free of charge. I often use this as a criterion because I believe it reflects the confidence of the vendor in the software program. It is certainly not a vote of confidence to say that a purchaser may obtain consultation about software use for a fee. However, it is a vote of confidence to say that the purchaser may call for assistance at any time and not be charged for such consultation.

Important here also is that often the practitioner will not be using this software, but rather the secretarial or administrative staff will be using it. Therefore, it is wise to include such individuals in the selection process and to seek their input and opinion. Such individuals will come to this process with a certain experience and expectations. Just as in clinical practice, it would be unwise to ignore such preconceptions and expectations of the "client."

It is important to limit one's expectations as to what a billing system can do. The system should perform billing and related services, but it should not be seen, for instance, as also capable of keeping track of all client information including assessment results, treatment plans, progress notes, and so on. Perhaps the most common pitfall of the novice is to attempt to have one or very few programs fulfill all of their various needs. This approach is unwise and one learns quickly that it is better to have several software programs, each performing well a specific need, rather than to have one large program imperfectly attempting to meet these diverse needs.

The best sources of initial information for billing programs are the advertisements in the *APA Monitor* and similar outlets. Such programs are highly specialized and it is doubtful that one would be able to find such programs or information about them in the typical retail computer store. At minimum, I would suggest the procurement of the user's manual associated with a particular billing system prior to its purchase. Most reputable vendors will permit such a purchase at a nominal cost and refund the purchase price of the manual when the software is purchased. Any reluctance to furnish such user's manuals or to provide detailed information or copies of actual printouts of statements and reports prior to purchase should be looked upon with great skepticism and caution. Almost without exception, I would advise avoiding a vendor with this type of noncooperative position. While such software programs are complex and often quite large, they are not, in the grand scheme of things, difficult programs for a reasonably proficient programmer. Thus, there are a sufficient number of such programs being advertised that one should certainly "shop around" for one that meets the requirements at the lowest cost. However, inquire prior to purchase whether there is a provision for update for your particular software program. As insurance forms change or other reporting requirements are altered, it would be necessary to obtain from the vendor either a new program or an update to your current program in order for it to continue to be functional. Again, as a rough guide, most reputable vendors who are experienced in the software business will have a policy concerning software update and will advise you of the cost. If a vendor has no existing policy or is evasive concerning cost, it would be a good indication to seek another vendor.

FINANCIAL MANAGEMENT

There are two distinct levels of financial management—personal and business—for which appropriate software can be of great benefit. For the individual who has a small, part-time private practice or who does consulting work or who is salaried in an academic position, management of personal finances can range from very simple (balancing a checkbook and filing a simple tax return each year) to more complex management of income from a variety of secondary sources such as investments and dividends. Further, it is important to track a myriad of work-related deductions, such as attendance at conferences, purchase of books, and travel expenses. For this first level there are a number of popular and easy-to-use software packages for personal financial management. These are, in essence, highly specialized data bases that permit entry of information concerning various checking accounts, savings accounts, personal assets, such as a home, cars, office furniture, stamp collections, and so on, as well as various liabilities, such as loans, mortgages, credit card accounts, and so on. The moderately priced packages (in the $100 to $200 price range) will most likely meet these needs. However, if the particular financial situation is complex, it is appropriate to review the user's manual to determine the specific parameters of the program. One can also invest in the relatively small cost of having an accountant review the needs and assist in the selection and in setting up the software package.

Although easy to use, these financial management packages are "blank slates" at the start. That is, you must set up the system by specifying, as an example, the number of different checking accounts, each credit card account, and the types of categories in which to record expenses, such as food, clothing, entertainment, gasoline, utilities, books, travel, medical, dental, and so on. Thus, there is some degree of planning necessary and the program will not ensure the accuracy of your financial condition. It will perform the calculations correctly based on the information given. If you have an existing system for personal management that is useful and effective for you, then its translation to the software program will be quite easy. If, however, you find your finances are disorganized and you do not keep good records, then the utilization of such a program will either serve as a stimulus for proper structure and accuracy and thus be beneficial, or will make matters infinitely worse by adding more chaos to your existing nonsystematic approach.

The second level of finance management software is appropriate for small businesses or group practices. In this instance, one is looking at a general ledger-type system of either a single-entry or double-entry format. Here it is imperative to have the advice of an accountant to help prepare the specific parameters to be entered into the computer system. The accounting programs that are available can range in cost from $200 to several thousand dollars and are distinguished by their complexity and flexibility. Some are complete packages that have all the various subcomponents while others are modular allowing one to add only the accounting functions necessary at a particular point in time. Here one should clearly include the administrator or bookkeeper who will be utilizing this software, as accounting is (at least from my perspective) an art rather than a science. The software must be flexible enough to meet the needs of the particular user, but also be complex enough to perform all the required functions as well as the cross-validation of information entered. The standards that were applied to billing software vendors clearly should be in effect. Accounting software programs are so complex that assistance is almost invariably required either from the retail outlet where it was purchased or from the vendor. The presence of an 800 telephone number is very important as well as a systematic program for periodic update to the software package. As a general rule of thumb, the use of such major accounting software should be attempted only after a manual system has been in place and has been proven to be effective. A major accounting package is a good example of software that should not be used to create order and systemization. This software should be used to increase the efficiency of an already validated and useful system.

BUDGET PREPARATION/ EXPENSE PROJECTIONS

One mundane task that is both important and tedious is the preparation of budgets, whether for a research grant or the operation of a group practice. A useful tool for this task is software known as "spreadsheets."

This highly specialized form of software combines aspects of a data base and a sophisticated calculator. A spreadsheet program is best conceptualized as simply a large sheet of paper with many rows and columns. The computer screen serves as a "window" on this large sheet of paper and can display any given subsection, but not the entire sheet, at any one time. By utilizing certain commands, one moves this window to position it over any specific location on this imaginary large sheet of paper. The rows and columns form a matrix and within this matrix, in any particular cell, either text or numbers can be placed. Additionally, formulas can be placed in any cell in order to perform calculations.

As a simple example, suppose a budget is being prepared for an imaginary psychology department in which each faculty member is allocated a certain amount of funds each semester in order to conduct teaching and research programs. On this spread sheet, you might place the name of each faculty member across the first row. Then vertically, in a column to the left of the first faculty member's name, you would assign certain labels, such as class A, class B, class C, lab A, lab B, to indicate teaching allocation. You would then construct a formula, for instance, that for each undergraduate student in a standard lecture class, $.50 was allocated for teaching materials, and for laboratory courses, $2.00 was allocated for each student. Then a column would be set aside under each faculty member to contain the number of students enrolled in the various courses and a second column would result from the multiplication of the student allotment by the student enrollment indicating a dollar amount. Finally, the teaching allocation row would be calculated by the sum of the individual columns associated with each faculty member who had individual class allocations. This type of system permits entry of simple information, such as the number of students enrolled, and then as each number is entered, all fields are recalculated and the result can be seen on the screen. This becomes useful when creating models or simulations. For instance, in preparing to discuss departmental budget needs with the administration, you could determine what type of formula for teaching assistance was feasible and then quickly calculate the bottom line budget. In like manner, if provided with a certain budget amount, you could attempt different formulas and observe the effect on specific allocation for various faculty.

This is a simple example, but a spreadsheet can be a powerful tool in preparing more complex budgets where one is allocating salaries, determining fringe benefits, direct and indirect costs, and making decisions across a number of budget years. A spreadsheet easily permits the "what if" type of analysis that is so necessary in budget preparation.

Spreadsheets can also be used for functions that are not financial. For instance, in attempting to match subjects on a number of different parameters, a spreadsheet is useful as it permits the easy "grouping" of subjects into different clusters and also permits the observation of the effect

```
File: EXAMPLE                    REVIEW/ADD/CHANGE              Escape: Main Menu
=======A=========B==========C==========D==========E==========F=========G======
  1!          Romanczyk              Jones              Smith
  2!          4students    allocation  students  allocation  students allocation
  3!             2
  4!class A         50     $100.00      200     $400.00        0       $0.00
  5!class B         25      $50.00      150     $300.00        0       $0.00
  6!class C          0       $0.00        0       $0.00        0       $0.00
  7!lab A           15      $60.00        0       $0.00       25     $100.00
  8!lab B            0       $0.00        0       $0.00       20      $80.00
  9!
 10!SUM          90.00     $210.00      350     $700.00       45     $180.00
 11!
 12!telepho    $150.00               $150.00              $150.00
 13!post       $100.00               $100.00              $100.00
 14!xerox      $225.00               $875.00              $112.50
 15!sum        $475.00             $1,125.00              $362.50
 16!
 17!TOTAL                  $685.00             $1,825.00              $542.50
 18!BUDGET   $3,052.50
---------------------------------------------------------------------------------
B18:  (Value, Layout-D2)  @SUM(C17+E17+G17)

Type entry or use @ commands                                        @-? for Help
```

```
                                                                    Page  1
     File:   EXAMPLE

            Romanczyk              Jones              Smith
            4students    allocation  students  allocation  students allocation
               2
     class A     50     $100.00      200     $400.00        0       $0.00
     class B     25      $50.00      150     $300.00        0       $0.00
     class C      0       $0.00        0       $0.00        0       $0.00
     lab A       15      $60.00        0       $0.00       25     $100.00
     lab B        0       $0.00        0       $0.00       20      $80.00

     SUM      90.00     $210.00      350     $700.00       45     $180.00

     telepho  $150.00               $150.00              $150.00
     post     $100.00               $100.00              $100.00
     xerox    $225.00               $875.00              $112.50
     sum      $475.00             $1,125.00              $362.50

     TOTAL               $685.00             $1,825.00              $542.50
     BUDGET  $3,052.50
```

FIGURE 5.1. A typical spreadsheet display. The top portion is the display seen on the CRT and the lower portion as it would appear on a print-out.

this has on group statistics. There are indeed a variety of applications for a spreadsheet and in fact some creative individuals have used it for accounting purposes, mailing lists, and even data bases. However, caution should be exercised here. Spreadsheet programs are designed specifically for "what if" situations and probably should be restricted to those. It is often tempting to utilize a powerful program as an all-purpose tool, but in general, this tendency should be avoided. It results in a misperception of efficiency and typically delays the acquisition of appropriate software that will more directly and efficiently address the problem at hand.

Chapter 6
Word Processing

OVERVIEW

A word processor is a software program that combines features of an ultra-sophisticated typewriter and a typesetting machine. The user enters text in a manner similar to that when using a typewriter, except that the program permits rapid editing of this information on the CRT and typically results in greatly improved efficiency. At minimum a good word processor should permit the setting of:

1. left and right margins
2. left and right justification
3. line spacing
4. top and bottom margins
5. pagination
6. headers and footers
7. multiple tabs
8. allow for inserting and deleting, as well as moving and copying, words or blocks of material
9. permit search and replace functions.

The search and replace function allows one to look for a particular word or component of a word and replace it with a different word or portion of a word in each instance found. For example, one could search for the name Mr. Smith and change it to Ms. Jones every time it occurs in the text. This can be very useful in manuscript preparation. If certain references are not known when preparing a manuscript draft, one could devise a simple system of using R1, R2, and so on to designate missing references. Later, when the references are known, the search and replace function can be used to substitute the correct references wherever they appear in the document. The search function alone is useful to find all instances of a particular reference throughout a manuscript.

A word processor is generally not functional for producing short letters and memos. If the material is less than one page, it is often easier to type in the traditional fashion. However, a word processor becomes extremely efficient when documents are rather long, such as a journal manuscript or when standard forms or correspondence need slight alterations in order to personalize them, as in the case of a form letter for requesting release of information. Because the word processor permits rapid editing and the ability to "cut and paste" pieces of documents, it allows for easier expression of creativity because the writer is able to produce a clean working document with very little time cost associated with making changes. Working with long documents that have pencil insertions, attached pages, and cross-outs is tedious and irritating. The word processor makes this a much more tolerable task, and many individuals who begin using the word processor find it difficult to go back to the traditional writing process, because it seems cumbersome and inefficient.

REPORTS

Perhaps one of the most tedious but important administrative tasks is the production of reports. Depending on the specific purpose of the report, the audience for which it is intended, and the services that have been provided, most professionals adopt a characteristic style and phraseology in their reports. Some degree of standardization is certainly desirable, because it permits the adoption of a structure that can enhance the clarity of the reports as well as ease the task of producing the report. A word processor is very useful for this task because it permits an appropriate blend of standardization and individualization.

Several years ago in a clinic I direct for learning disabled and hyperactive children, the burden for writing progress reports for each of the children became excessive. The remediation programs designed for certain academic subjects were detailed and too long to be incorporated into reports. However, since the reports were to be used by parents and teachers to help assist in the child's academic activities, it was important that such detail be included. The solution to this dilemma was to use a word processor. We chose a word processor program known as Word Star to be used on one of our Northstar Advantage microcomputers. This microcomputer is a desk top model with dual floppy disks and has the CP/M operating system.

The staff analyzed what was currently in the reports, what was desirable to add to the reports, and the specific individualized goal plans that were conducted with the children. An outline and structure was produced for our new reports and each procedure utilized was described in some detail. Of course, each procedure was not used with each child and thus we were assembling a library of specific procedures. A face page was created with certain basic identifying information such as the child's name, address,

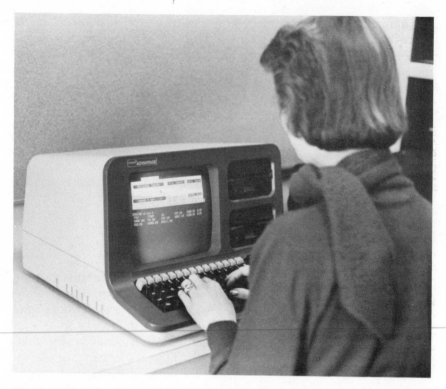

FIGURE 6.1. A word processing station utilizing a high-density disk storage system. This is a good example of an "all-in-one" type desk top computer.

date of birth, date of report, number of sessions attended, and so on. This was stored as one file. Then, each separate description of specific procedures was stored as a unique file, which resulted in many scores of such files. Each file was then given a unique code number. The code numbers and corresponding file name comprised an index page, which served as a reference for our library of individual descriptions.

Now, report writing is a relatively easy process. A staff member simply indicates by number which components will comprise the report and these are assembled using Word Star. First a file is created for the report for a specific child, and then the specific individual descriptions are entered sequentially. Word Star, as is true for many word processing programs, has the ability to append different files to the current working file. Thus, rather than laboriously retyping the descriptive paragraph concerning the general procedure for sight vocabulary drill of Dolch words at the second-grade level, the user simply indicates that she wants to append file 23. This is done by pressing a combination of three keys on the keyboard and the number 23. The word processor then retrieves these paragraphs and places them in the proper sequence. When the entire document is assembled, it is edited for changes that are unique to the particular child. The author is then able to devote more time to the important task of integrating this information and presenting her observations and conclusions. Thus, while there is no time saving in this latter activity, a great deal of time is saved in producing the standard part of the report, the part that describes what was done. In terms of cost benefit, this type of approach has produced documents that are very well received by the parents, are significantly more detailed and extensive than was previously the case, and also are produced in half the time it took to produce previously less detailed reports.

A similar procedure can be adopted for writing standardized assessment reports. These reports are primarily written for school psychologists and Committees on the Handicapped and thus, detail is desirable. Starting with a standard assessment battery, including tests such as the WISC-R, the Vineland Social Maturity Scale, Key Math, the Woodcock Reading Mastery Test, and so on, descriptive paragraphs are created for each test to explain its purpose and administration. In addition, for each test the particular subscore categories are indicated with the values left blank. Therefore the user can simply retrieve the descriptions for the various tests administered, place them in the proper order, and then fill in the specific scores. Space is also reserved for comments about each student's testing behavior. Finally, an interpretive summary of tests administered as well as recommendations based on the assessments is produced by the examiner that is clearly unique for each child. As in the above example the quality and reception of the reports increases dramatically with a concomitant decrease in preparation time compared to previous methods.

Thus, for clinical applications, without question, a word processor is perhaps the single most important piece of software. It permits not only the general production of correspondence, manuscripts, and other documents, but it also permits a degree of control and specificity of report writing that is highly desirable and highly efficient. It is often found that when much of the tedium of report writing is eliminated, individuals will spend more time on important interpretive and summary portions, because they do not have to devote as much time to the routine matters of simple document preparation.

OTHER USES

There are certainly many uses for a word processor. Documents, such as research protocols and procedures, staff training manuals, newsletters, client notes, and various questionnaires and behavior observation forms, that are constantly being revised are excellent candidates for the word processor. In particular, once a person is somewhat skilled in using the word processor, it is easy to construct forms and templates that previously took more time to create. For instance, in conducting behavior observations it is often useful to record behavior at small time intervals. Within each interval there is often a coding system of circling different letters or numbers that represent various behaviors. This system is rather straightforward, but it is often tedious to produce a recording form that basically consists of a series of small boxes, each of which contains the specific behavior codes. With a word processor, however, it is easy to construct one such interval and then repeatedly "copy" it horizontally across the page and then vertically. I have found that in this type of task, I can usually outperform a typist by a factor of 10 or better, and I must confess, I still use the hunt and peck method of typing. This advantage is even more pronounced when creating questionnaires or forms wherein the placement and format of questions are often juggled. Using the word processor to construct questionnaires takes about one-quarter the time it would take a skilled typist. Revisions and alterations become routine, low-cost tasks with respect to valuable support staff time.

BEWARE COMPULSIVE BEHAVIOR

Because a word processor makes easy the often difficult task associated with writing, it can produce an interesting side effect. One typically balances the desire for perfection and "attractive looking" paperwork with the time and effort involved in correcting mistakes, making minor changes, and visually arranging and rearranging the document. Since the word processor makes such activities quite easy, an illusion is produced that there is little time involved in these activities. I have heard many colleagues lament in private, and I have certainly admitted in public that I have often spent more time in producing a given document using a word processor than I would have if I had done it in the traditional fashion. This is particularly true when the document is a newsletter, questionnaire, or document that will be circulated on a wide basis. The document almost becomes a plaything; one tries various creative processes with the word processor and in essence, attempts to duplicate the professional results one sees from a publisher. Interestingly, it is indeed possible to duplicate many of these effects such as different-sized type, accenting various sections in bold print, changing pitch, margins, and so on. There is no question that the documents produced in this fashion are far more appealing than those produced in the traditional fashion, but it is not necessarily true that they are "better." This is a decision that each user will make for themselves, depending upon the intended use of the document. Even though there is this tendency to pursue perfection, even minimal self-control procedures are usually adequate to properly balance the various influences.

SELECTION

Word processors vary greatly in the ease of use and sophistication as well as in cost. Prices range from $50 to $100, up to the range of $500 to $700. As this will be perhaps the most used software program, it is wise to carefully evaluate the various programs available. I strongly suggest that one not be too influenced by ease of use, as often this can be accomplished only by a compromise in the flexibility and scope of the software. Be forewarned that most word processors do not easily handle our APA style for references. Also, be sure that the options available for your word processor can, in fact, be utilized by your microcomputer system. As an example, Word Star is a powerful word processing program that can be run on virtually all the popular microcomputers. However, it is not the case that all of Word Star's functions can be utilized on each of these microprocessors. Clearly the easiest way to assess a word processing package is to ask to try it out at a computer retail store. This is not an imposition to such a store, because word processors are perhaps the most frequently sold software package, so computer retail stores should have demonstration copies of many different types. Certainly, bring with you some examples of the type of documents you wish to produce and then either ask the sales representative to enter them for you or enter them yourself after a brief lesson on how to use the word processor. Since the choice of any particular piece of software is always a compromise between various factors, the only way to resolve this problem is to test it yourself or accept advice from a colleague who is having success with a particular piece of software. However, even in this latter case, be sure to determine that you are attempting to produce documents that are similar to those of your colleague. What works well for one person may not be advantageous to another even though you may be engaged in ostensibly similar activities.

PRINTERS

One factor associated with the selection of word processing software is the type of printer that will be utilized. For most individuals, the choice is between a dot matrix printer and a letter-quality printer. These two choices have quite different consequences with respect to both speed and cost as well as to print quality.

As mentioned previously, the dot matrix printer constructs characters similar to the image seen on the video display. Therefore, its flexibility is high and with the proper software, it can accurately reproduce whatever is on the video display. Since the letter-quality printers use a mechanical system similar to a typewriter, each letter, number, or symbol has its own specific location on the print wheel surface. As such, it cannot produce graphics or special effects such as changing type sizes. Therefore, for maximum flexibility, a dot matrix printer is highly recommended. With respect to word processing, it not only permits construction of drafts at high speed, but it also permits the construction of forms, questionnaires, and other materials that require specialized and varied type faces and type sizes as well as graphics. Thus if letter quality is required, it is highly desirable to have both a dot matrix printer and a letter-quality printer for your microcomputer system. One can switch back and forth between the two printers by removing and reinserting the cables connected to each printer. A preferable approach would be to use an operating system that can easily handle multiple printers. The software simply directs the output to either of the desired printers. At first this might seem extravagant, but it is less expensive to purchase a good quality dot matrix printer and a relatively low speed, letter-quality printer than to purchase a high speed, letter-quality printer. It is important here to point out that the terms, *low speed* and *high speed*, are relative and cannot be compared between the two printers. A dot matrix printer typically has a speed in the 80 to 200 characters per second range, whereas for typical letter-quality printers, 55 characters per second represents the practical upper limit. Thus, spending several thousand dollars on a "high speed" letter-quality printer represents a greater expenditure than purchasing a dot matrix printer in the 100 character per second range and a letter-quality printer in the 20 character per second range.

If graphics are not an important function, then a different approach can be taken. There are devices known as printer buffers and software programs termed spoolers that permit information that will be printed to be temporarily stored either on disk or in reserve memory. This information will in turn be passed on to the printer. The advantage of this is that the CPU can transmit this information either to disk or to memory at a speed far in excess of the printer's speed of operation. By doing this the CPU then frees itself of this information and can go on to other tasks without waiting for the printer to finish. The hardware and software that are a part of the spooler or buffer then take the information that is being temporarily stored and they transmit it to the printer at the printer's speed of operation. Especially for a relatively slow, letter-quality printer, this represents a great savings in time when viewing overall computer usage and efficiency. In essence, buffering or spooling compensates for slow printers. Thus, it appears that one is using the computer for two separate purposes:

first, to continue with a particular software program, such as working on a second document or on an entirely different activity, and, second, to print the first document at the same time. There are some word processors that have a built-in version of a spooler which transmits information from a disk file to a printer and links this operation with the user's current operations on the word processor. This can result in a quite noticeable reduction in speed to the user. As an example, in the middle of typing a sentence, the keyboard may appear to go dead as the computer is taking information from a disk file, transferring it to a memory buffer area, which in turn transmits it to the printer. If one is printing relatively short documents, this is a minor inconvenience and should not be of concern. However, in producing manuscripts or a great deal of paper work during the course of the day, such low-level spoolers are quite an annoyance.

If one decides to take the approach of maximizing the efficiency of the computer (and, in fact, in some cases this can even obviate the need to purchase a second computer in a busy office), a buffer is an excellent choice. A buffer is a hardware device that has its own RAM and built-in software in ROM. It "looks" like a printer to the computer, but it can communicate with the computer at very high speed, many times faster than even a very high-speed printer and can also send its data to the printer at the printer's pace. It is important to choose a buffer or spooler that has a memory capacity equal in size to the majority of the documents being produced. That is, if the majority of word processing involves documents of only a half dozen pages at a time, then an 8K buffer is usually quite sufficient. As the documents grow larger, one may need a 32K or even a 64K buffer.

In general, I recommend the printer buffer approach as opposed to the spooler. The reason is simple. From the user's point of view the buffer is easy to operate, as there are no software changes. The computer "thinks" it is sending information to the printer as the printer buffer "looks" (that is, electronically) just like a printer. With a spooler, there are often intermediary steps of creating disk files and, in a sense, assisting in the management of the system. It is not difficult, but it is simply an unnecessary additional burden. The current cost of printer buffers is quite low, and in many cases one can purchase a basic unit that can be enlarged (i.e., one can add more memory to it) as needed. A printer buffer has greatly enhanced the productivity in my administrative office and has produced a three-fold efficiency in the preparation of clinical reports and habilitative goal plans. Further, although the context here has been word processing, a printer buffer functions with *any* program that transmits information to the printer.

Chapter 7
Data Bases

OVERVIEW

A data base is a collection of information or data that is organized in a specific format so that individual elements of the collection can be retrieved and processed. In one sense, a telephone book is a good example of a data base. It has contained within it names, addresses, and phone numbers, and one can find a person quite easily by entering the section that corresponds to the person's last name. However, the phone book permits retrieval in only one format: by last name. Thus it is appropriate for only a highly specialized use—that of finding the telephone number for a particular person. Computer data bases are far more flexible and permit a wider range of utility. In a typical data base, one establishes a file which contains data concerning particular categories of information. For instance, one might have a file of references that is being used to prepare a manuscript, or a file containing client information used to establish patterns of care in a private practice, or a file containing students' academic history, including course performance. Each file is composed of individual records; a record is a collection of individual pieces of information that are of the same categories for each entry (record) in the file. Each record, in turn, is composed of individual fields (pieces) of information. In a simple data base of names, addresses, and phone numbers, the fields would be composed of the last name, first name, address, town, state, zip code, and telephone number. A record would then be the information for one person from each of these fields which are stored in the computer. Each record will have a sequential number associated with it and a specific place in the storage file. In turn, a file is the collection of the individual records.

FILE-ORIENTED DATA BASE

There are many different types of data bases and perhaps the simplest and easiest to use is the file-oriented data base. In the example above there are individual records, each of which are of the same format and are stored in a sequential manner in a file. Unlike the telephone book example, however, one can retrieve this information typically by indexing according to any given field within a record. Thus, one may sort a file by choosing a particular field, such as last names, and arranging all the records into alphabetical order. Then when a print-out is requested, all the names will appear neatly organized as in the telephone book. However, if one was conducting a bulk mailing, for example, and wished the names sorted by zip code in order to take advantage of lower postal rates, then one would sort on zip code and the file would be organized according to this field. One could similarly do the same for street address, town, state, or even telephone number. Our simple record could be altered somewhat to contain also a field to signify birthday and a field for gift, where it could be indicated whether a card or present was sent in recognition of each person's birthday. One could then sort this information and ask for, in a given month, all the individuals who had a birthday that month for whom a card or gift was to be sent. One could also extend this to ask for all individuals in the state of Pennsylvania who have a birthday in December to whom a card is to be sent.

This simple example, of course, would not be a very functional use of a data base. It simply illustrates the type of information that can be retrieved and the importance of determining a priori what information is important and how that information is to be combined into reports. It is important for each record to designate a key field, which is a field that serves to index the file. In most cases last name is chosen as the key field. In some clinical settings or research settings where confidentiality must be preserved, a key field might be a consecutive client number, or a code number on a research questionnaire.

In many ways, the file-oriented data base is similar to an index card system. That is, on each card one usually has a place for certain pieces of information and then designates a key by which index cards are stored in a file box. An index card file of journal articles often contains authors' names, title, journal, year, volume number, page number, and abstract. In a manual index card system the key field is usually first author's last name and the other information is placed on different lines of the index card. Again, the problem with this type of indexing is that one cannot readily search by title, topic, or journal. For this reason in most libraries one will find an index card system for title, one for topic, and one for last name. This type of system is redundant. With a simple data base on a microcomputer, one would enter the same information from the index card, but since each field can be sorted and searched, and only the output or reports differ, the information need only be entered once. That is, one may construct a report format to print a list of all references by author, a second report to print all references alphabetized by topic areas, and perhaps a third report that might print a report on all articles concerning a particular topic that has been published in the journal, *Behavior Therapy*, since 1972.

Thus, most tasks that currently utilize an index card system lend themselves to a file-oriented data base. Such data bases also tend to be the least expensive and the easiest to learn to use.

COMPLEX DATA BASES

One common drawback of simple, file-oriented data-base programs is that they do not permit numerical manipulation of data and can be quite slow. Typically there is limited report generation in such programs and it is not uncommon to discover that one must purchase the file portion of the data base and a separate report generation section. The more complex data bases, however, are better integrated and permit a wider range of functioning. For instance, if one was preparing a data base on student information, it might contain the name, address, and telephone number but also include social security number, declared major, academic advisor, requirements completed, and grade for each course taken. For such a data base it would be desirable to have information such as overall GPA and major GPA calculated. While this might seem a simple task, some data bases will do it easily and others not at all or with great difficulty. One important function to discriminate when evaluating data bases is whether or not they can perform on-screen calculations. The task of adding the current course grades (in numerical format, not letter grades), dividing the sum by the number of courses taken and having this appear on the screen as each record is inspected, will not be possible for all data bases. However, the majority of data bases perform this type of task off-line. That is, in preparing a printed report, the records are searched and the calculations are performed at that time and then printed. This example is good for determining specifically how the data base will be used. If one is engaged in academic advising and has students drop in to discuss their progress, it would be desirable to have a data base that permits on-screen analysis, as it is swift. However, if the task is more administrative, then this type of on-screen function is not necessary. Several years ago, when I served as director of clinical training, I designed a data base using a commercial program which did not incorporate on-screen calculations. However, this was not an impediment as my purpose was very focused: to provide APA with the various reports necessary for annual review and site visit. The data base was updated in cycles, typically at the end of a semester, and then specific reports were printed as necessary. This type of analysis—to ascertain what information is to be stored, how the reports are to be constructed, and how much of the information needs to be analyzed and placed on the screen—is an important one, not only from the point of view of designing an efficient and useful system, but also in determining the cost of a system. Data bases can range in price from under $100 to several thousand dollars.

Another characteristic of certain sophisticated data bases is the ability to construct defined fields. That is, as an example for our student records, it would be somewhat tedious to enter for each student each of the various fields for department code, course title, credit hours, and instructor (e.g., "PSY 349, Behavior Disorders of Childhood, 4 credits, R. G. Romanczyk"). However, such information that is fixed or at least not often changed, can in one sense be seen as a small data base in and of itself. Some data bases can allow for such sub-data bases, wherein one would enter into a field "PSY 350." Once this is entered, a secondary data base would be searched and the information corresponding to it, such as course title, number of credit hours, and instructor would be retrieved and automatically placed within the appropriate fields of the current record. This is not only a time saving device, but also permits a reduction in user errors. For example, in my case, having had a long history of viewing quite amazing permutations to the spelling of my last name, I would be far more confident in searching a data base to ascertain which students are registered for my courses if this information has been automatically entered into a field rather than having the various computer operators enter my name manually into the instructor field for each student. As information that is to be entered into an individual record becomes extensive and redundant with respect to specific cross-references, this type of automatic fill function in a data base becomes extremely useful and desirable. If one were to attempt to construct a client billing system using a data base rather than a self-contained billing program, this type of function becomes a necessity.

RELATIONAL DATA BASES

The newest generation of data-base programs allows even more flexibility than outlined above. In particular, programs referred to as relational data bases permit the data from separate files to be accessed simultaneously. That is, one may have several different files, perhaps one concerning client progress notes, a second with client demographics, and a third with assessment information. These data bases can be utilized to access individual portions of records from these divergent files and to prepare specific reports. While these are perhaps the most powerful of the data bases available today, they are also typically the most difficult to utilize. For example, a powerful data base, produced by Ashton-Tate, is dBaseII. If there currently is a standard for data bases, this particular one probably is it. It is in very wide usage for countless different applications. However, it is not unusual for the nonprogrammer to spend several hundred hours becoming familiar with the data base and constructing a system for his particular needs. There are seminars offered nationally that spend three full days acquainting the user with this very powerful software program. Thus, once again, it is important to ascertain one's specific needs and to balance the power and capability of the program with the acquisition time necessary to learn its functions. In many cases it may be far more efficient to utilize a simple file-oriented data base to grant that there will be redundancy across different files, but to know that acquisition time will be just a few hours and thus the overall savings may be quite substantial.

THE NEWEST GENERATION
OF DATA BASES

There are currently a few data bases that are user-friendly and allow one to enter information in a field-free format. That is, there are no preset fields. If one wanted to enter client notes, reflections about a manuscript that was just read, or notes concerning a student's performance in class, one enters this information just as on a word processor. This information is still stored as individual records, but when information must be retrieved, one would request it by saying "give me everything about client Jones" or "give me everything about Romanczyk's 1984 article on microcomputers." The advantage to this type of data base is extreme ease of use and great flexibility. However, it is not appropriate for producing structured reports. Because the information is entered in an unstructured format, one cannot readily impose a report structure upon it. It is much like a memorandum file, but instead of searching laboriously for a given memorandum by examining the entire file cabinet, this type of system looks for key words such as a person's name, a date, or a phrase. Because of this, the search is imprecise and often produces extraneous information. Ironically, this type of data base is more useful for the skilled user because it permits a degree of flexibility not found in the more sophisticated data bases, and relies on the user to compensate for its lack of structure. Even though this type of data base may appear attractive in advertising or in demonstrations, it still should probably not be the first choice of the novice.

Recently some sophisticated data bases have appeared that combine all the data-base functions mentioned to this point. However, for the most part, this new generation of programs still requires sophistication on the user's part. Although they can appear user-friendly in the final format, they require a substantial amount of programming. That is, many of the data bases are actually a self-contained, programming language. They have specific commands and syntax that must be learned and then utilized in order to write the data-base programs. They are, of course, far more powerful than the more generic languages such as BASIC and PASCAL. Nevertheless, they require a substantial amount of effort to utilize, and some degree of sophistication on the user's part to construct the algorithms that are necessary for the data base to function properly. At present, although sophisticated data bases are difficult to use, some factors are changing. As microcomputers are beginning to permit routinely greater and greater storage capacity as well as large amounts of RAM (approximately .5 meg), software developers can create extremely large programs that compensate for user inexperience and permit sophistication that was not possible just a year or two ago. This trend is readily seen in the new Apple Macintosh and IBM PC-XT and AT microcomputers. Given this sophisticated hardware and extensive memory capabilities, there has begun a whole new evolution of software development that will soon be available to the average user.

SPECIALIZED DATA BASES

Up to this point, all the examples have concerned generic data bases, that is, data bases that the user configures to her own purposes. One could take these data-base programs and construct separate data bases for one's coin collection, clients, subjects in a chronic outcome study, or favorite ethnic food recipes, all using the same software program. There are many other data bases, however, that have a specialized purpose that do not allow the user to make any alterations in the programs. Such software programs have the advantage of being very user-friendly and highly efficient, if it precisely matches the specific need.

One good example is bibliographic data bases. That is, APA has established a specific set of guidelines for the preparation of manuscript references. Given this, there are a number of programs available that permit the cataloging of reference material. One enters information about journal articles, books, conference presentations, and so on in a standard format. Some of these programs include the ability to specify key words and enter abstracts. Thus, one can retrieve information in a manner that is very similar to the method described above, but can also have this information printed out in standard APA format. Such programs are usually an excellent investment. At some point we have all constructed reading lists or reference lists using index cards and scraps of paper. Often, such repeated activities bear a striking resemblance to one another with respect to the information being collated. Therefore, there is an excellent match between the needs associated with this type of activity and the specific bibliographic data bases available. One simply inspects the promotional material or user's manual to determine if there is a match in format and purpose. I have a strong conditioned aversion to manual index card bibliographic filing systems, as I find them painfully slow and never organized in a fashion that I find useful across situations. In contrast, a computer system is almost (but not quite) enjoyable to use. Its flexibility in searching and printing references relieves much of the tedium of writing.

Chapter 8
Assessment and Diagnosis*

AUTOMATED SCORING

For many years, there have been commercial services that will score the results of numerous standardized tests. Perhaps the most outstanding example is computer scoring of the MMPI. One sends the questionnaire or data sheet to the service and usually within 24 to 48 hours the service returns the results. There are many advantages to this type of computerized scoring assistance. First, if one is managing a large number of such test administrations, there is clear savings in time and a reduction in the drudgery of manual scoring. Second, there is typically a gain made in accuracy. However, for the individual who administers such tests only infrequently, the savings are not present and the use of a computer is not cost effective.

A distinction must be made between automated scoring and automated interpretation. For the first, the computer simply matches the information contained in the test administration manual to the test responses and computes the appropriate scores. This is a relatively easy task from a programming point of view. In fact, it is quite common to find individual users who write their own programs to do this type of automated scoring. In particular, questionnaire results lend themselves easily to such scoring as do many of the self-report inventories. Often, scoring requires assigning various numerical weights to each response or clustering responses into categories. The computer is a fine tool for this type of task and can perform at high speed. However, the major drawback is the time needed to enter the information into the computer. Most sophisticated testing services use an optical scanner to read the responses on the test booklet. Such devices are expensive and are usually beyond the budget of the average microcomputer user. As an alternative, one can retype the responses into the computer using the test booklet as a template. This task is tedious, can result in error, and can greatly reduce the cost–benefit ratio. On the

*This chapter was coauthored by Stephanie Lockshin and Raymond Romanczyk.

other hand, if the test information is to be used for research purposes and collected for many individuals, this type of entry into the computer can be beneficial, because complex analyses can then be performed. In this regard, such entry of test information is not different than keypunching one's data. However, in such instances the purpose is quite specific. It is not to obtain clinical information concerning a given individual, but rather collecting information across many individuals. Thus, it is important to weigh the time and effort necessary to place the information into the computer with the utility of information that will be provided.

The line of software available through American Guidance Services that matches several of the assessment instruments they market is a good example of highly efficient computer programs that require manual entry of test responses. Computer scoring software is available for the Woodcock Reading Mastery Test, the Kaufman Assessment Battery for Children, and the new revised Vineland Adaptive Behavior Scales. Like many achievement or intellectual assessment tests, these are characterized by using a series of tables to convert raw scores to scaled scores, standardized scores, age equivalents, and so on. This process can be laborious because raw scores are being used with a number of tables and composite indices. The particular software for these three packages is similar in that one enters the relatively few raw scores associated with each instrument. The software then calculates all the various scores and statistics and presents them in a format similar to the one that would result if the task had been done manually. Further, in the version for the Woodcock Reading Mastery Test, the software stores the information and sets up a file for each child. When future test results are entered, the software can compute pre/post scores for the individual as well as statistics concernng class averages and rankings. To use such a program for only the occasional scoring of such a test would not be very efficient, although it usually is more fun to do it this way.

For my own use (RGR) in directing a clinic for learning disabled children, the Woodcock in particular is used with great frequency. Hand scoring had, of course, always been the norm for us until a few years ago when we obtained the computer-assisted scoring software. The impact has been quite impressive, as the results of our pre/post testing sessions are available more quickly and with a much lower frequency of scoring error. We are also provided with information that is very useful for overall program evaluation. That is, previously, if one wished group totals, ranking, means, etc., this was a separate process distinct from the scoring of the test itself. Now by using the computer, scoring the test and preparing group information are, in fact, the same process. Given the criteria mentioned before, this is an excellent example of the utility of using a microcomputer on a routine basis for certain tasks. One obtains a variety of information from a one-step process rather than from a manual multiple-step process.

INTERPRETATION

Computerized interpretation of test results is a distinct area in itself. In this application, the same information is obtained as for computerized scoring but then a second step is instituted. According to a specific algorithm or formula, descriptors are attached to the test results, and interpretations and conclusions drawn. Once again, the MMPI is the prototype for this type of computer interpretation. Programs are readily available on microcomputer systems for interpretive scoring for instruments such as the MMPI, WISC-R, WAIS, Bender-Gestalt, 16PF, and Rorschach. From a research perspective, the use of such programs is very interesting and could be used to examine more fully the decision-making process used by clinicians. However, there are important cautions that must be raised if the intent is to use such software for individual, client-centered decisions in the clinical process. The professional issues will be discussed further in chapter 14. The technical issues involve the process of attempting to use a microcomputer to perform functions such as drawing conclusions from test scores. The provision of such information, along with specific recommendations for clinical services often gives the illusion of a powerful system. This certainly seems true when one visits the various booths at professional conferences. An example often provided by the exhibitors would be to enter into the computer some very basic demographic information and perhaps WISC-R scores. They then very quickly receive a multi-page interpretive report with suggestions for further treatment, placement and the type of academic tasks the child should receive.

Questions should arise, especially for the novice computer user, on how these decisions are being made. Clearly, the software program simply contains a set of instructions that attach differential weight to various sub-scale items and also performs an analysis of the clustering of these items. Based upon both simple and complex formula, phrases and descriptors are chosen from a library that is part of the program based upon the specific scores and their patterns. In this way it is not significantly different from the examples described in chapter 6. In its simplest form it may be described as a matching task, that is, which score or combination of scores are associated with which descriptors and phrases. The computer performs a match and then lists "conclusions" in a prose format. Thus, the computer is clearly not necessarily presenting fact, state-of-the-art interpretation, or expert clinical judgement, but rather it is applying a formula and set of rules that was determined by the programmer. The accuracy and utility of the reports printed are a direct function of both the skill of the programmer in applying these algorithms and the knowledge and experience of the person (hopefully a skilled clinician) who provided the programmer with the various rules, phrases, and descriptors.

The state-of-the-art is quite good with respect to software that provides scoring for various tests. The reason is simply that there is a one-to-one correspondence between the functions the program performs and those that can be accomplished manually by using the test scoring manual. The purpose of such programs is to gain speed over the manual scoring procedures. However, software programs that provide interpretation are another matter, as interpretation rarely has a set of hard-and-fast rules. Thus the danger is the extension of simple but useful scoring programs to perform not only the manual aspects of assessment, but also to provide the summaries and conclusions. While many individuals who use such computer programs readily sing their praises and speak about the increased number of clients that they are able to serve, it is not clear if in fact the best interests of the client or of the profession are being served. One should be wary of these software programs, and should proceed with extreme caution and care. It is not difficult for a good programmer to create the illusion of competence, but it is quite another matter indeed to create a software program that can handle the myriad of information sources and duplicate the clinical judgement necessary when discussing the characteristics and needs of an *individual* client. As mentioned above, the potential for very exciting research is clear, but it is also clear that such systems are being directed primarily at clinical application and not research.

DIAGNOSIS

Many of the pros and cons discussed with respect to computer-assisted assessment are true for computer-assisted diagnosis. The great potential lies in viewing computer-assisted diagnosis as essentially the interface between the clinician who collects important pieces of information via interview, observation, history, and formal and informal assessment procedures, and the comparison of such information to a large data base of the specific criteria necessary to make a diagnosis. This book is not an appropriate forum for a discussion of the issues concerning diagnosis per se. Formal diagnosis is certainly an important activity for many psychologists, and the principles involved in computer-assisted diagnosis are easily extended to other systems of classification, because the process is one of decision making.

Much more progress has been made in medicine utilizing computers for diagnostic assistance. Medicine has a superior taxonomy and methodology of assessment than is currently available in clinical psychology or psychiatry. This allows for a more straightforward approach to giving specific weights to different factors or symptoms. In contrast, psychological diagnosis and classification tends to rely more heavily on subjective patterns and interactions, such that specific quantification of individual symptoms or behaviors does not have a corresponding impact as in medical diagnosis.

Currently there is little reason for optimism concerning accurate computer-assisted diagnosis, as the reliability between experienced clinicians and their diagnoses is not terribly impressive. Until diagnostic systems provide the specificity necessary to allow a high degree of reliability among experienced clinicians, then it would be futile to attempt accuracy with computer models. Indeed it is unclear what accuracy would mean because it is difficult to establish a standard. Thus, the diagnostic programs that appear for microcomputer use should be viewed with great skepticism, and their use could be deleterious to the clinical process. One appropriate function that the microcomputer can serve in the diagnostic process, and there is some software appearing now, is as a prompt to the diagnostician. Rather than entering specific information and receiving a diagnosis, the microcomputer program can emulate the structure of decision as outlined, for instance, in *DSM III*. There is an interaction between the user and computer as the computer serves to prompt for alternatives and possibilities, rather than to be used as a final authority. Such a computer system is simply a somewhat friendlier and more complex form of a paper-and-pencil checklist approach. What is clearly lacking, however, is any systematic research on such issues and for the moment, this activity is relevant from a research perspective, but should not be endorsed or taken seriously from a clinical perspective.

As research in the diagnostic and clinical decision-making processes continue, and as sophistication in computer modeling continues, it may indeed be the case that well-validated and useful software may be developed. However, this is predicated on substantial advances in both areas and thus, we would not see this development as imminent. In contrast, software designed to assist in prompting the clinician as to relevant information that should be collected is a more distinct possibility in the near future. We would view this in the same context as those interviewers who use a prepared outline of questions and topics to help structure an interview in order to insure that topics are covered objectively and that comprehensiveness of coverage is not inadvertently influenced by specific content revealed in the interview. Such prompts are very useful, especially when large amounts of information are being collected. In like manner, the computer can, in some regards, serve as a sophisticated colleague who can ask pertinent generic questions and help assemble all the information into logical units and clusters. One can view the development of such "diagnostic" software as an integration of current knowledge about data bases with the generally accepted standards on the type of clinical information that must be obtained in order to process the information in an efficient fashion. This is clearly one step short of actually making a diagnosis or judgement and we believe this is an important distinction which will be discussed further in later chapters.

REVIEW OF CURRENT RESEARCH

Johnson and Williams (1975) described a prototype on-line computer-admitting system, the Psychiatric Assessment Unit (PAU), for a Veteran's Administration hospital. The initial version of the PAU data processing system was programmed on a Control Data 3200 system (a mainframe computer).

The following is a brief summary of the testing process. Upon arrival to the facility, the capability of the client to complete the computerized self-report testing was assessed via a brief interview with the PAU coordinator. Eligible clients were given a mental status exam which followed the structured format of Spitzer and Endicott's (1969) Current and Past Psychopathology Scales. The interview was conducted by a staff person who entered the data into the computer during the course of the interview. Subsequently, a computer-derived narrative report including a *DSM III* diagnosis was produced. The client was then told how to complete the computerized assessment which consisted of a medical history questionnaire, the MMPI, Differential Personality Questionnaire, the Shipley Hartford Test for Intellectual Performance, the Briggs Social History, the Beck Depression Inventory, and a problem list. Upon completion of each test, the computer analyzed the responses and produced a narrative report. The data were then reviewed by the project staff and optimal treatment disposition for each client was determined.

Evaluation results indicated that in a 2-week period prior to PAU implementation, in-patient treatment staff spent 13.5% of their time conducting intake evaluation procedures. After the PAU was implemented, only 4% of staff time was expended in the intake process.

Another positive outcome due to implementation of the PAU system was an increase in the number of clients for whom some form of treatment was recommended at intake. Furthermore, as the system collects standardized clinical data at intake and at periodic follow-up, an extensive data base consisting of client characteristics, treatment programs, and progress is available to administrators. The authors suggested that this type of data base aids clinical administrators in designing treatment programs that are more appropriate to the needs of the clients.

Johnson, Giannetti, and Williams (1978) reported on the first commercially available system to make use of microcomputer technology in a mental health setting. Lab II, produced by Psych Systems, is a self-contained on-line microcomputer based psychological testing station located at the user site. Lab II is programmed to administer the following assessments: the Strong Campbell Vocational Interest Inventory, the Shipley-Hartford Intelligence scale, the MMPI, measures of arithmetic and memory ability, the Beck Depression and Hopelessness Inventory, and an index of test dissimulation (to assess client's ability to use the computer).

Byers (1981) discussed the implementation of a microcomputer testing system in a private clinical psychology practice. Byers indicated that the computer saved the client time, reduced errors due to the client becoming "out of synch" with the answer sheet and test booklet, and ensured that the client answered all of the questions. In addition, staff time required for scoring and interpretation was eliminated as these functions were carried out by the computer. The major weakness of the system identified by Byers was that it is only useful for screening given the range of the tests administered. Moreover, he found that some of the computer-prepared reports disagreed with clinical judgement.

Specialized Testing Capabilities

According to Johnson (1984) the most radical development in the area of computerized testing is "adaptive testing." This process involves a decision process based upon input to ascertain which questions should be asked of which persons. In other words, the computer is specifically programmed to pursue a particular sequence of questions (test items) based on the client's response to any given item.

Another development involves item construction. As a result of technological advances, radically different types of items are possible using the computer medium. For example, complex cognitive tasks could be presented via tachistoscopic presentations. Learning tasks could branch to various levels of difficulty, add or delete cues for correct responses, or provide various distractors. Such methods could be employed to assess an individual's capacity to learn or perform under various conditions. Roid and Gorsuch (1977) have suggested that computerized test administration programs would ideally present new assessment devices that are not possible with paper and pencil tests (e.g., complex memory or pattern recognition task, tailored testing of items or scales, or criterion referenced diagnostic tests).

Client Reactions to Computerized Assessment

Central to the evaluation of the efficacy of computers in clinical assessment is client reaction. Although most of the studies reviewed reported overall favorable reactions to the computer, the methodology employed to assess client reaction differed across the studies. Table 8.1 summarizes the various methods employed to date to assess client reactions to computerized assessment. A cursory glance at Table 8.1 underscores the fact that few systematic measures have been used. In addition, assessment measures are idiosyncratic to the particular study, which makes comparison across studies difficult. Also of interest is the fact that little attention has been given to identifying specific client characteristics. This line of research would perhaps lead to the ability to predict which clients would make better candidates for computer-administered assessment.

Elwood and Clark (1978), for example, assessed the reactions of 70 children (4–13 years old) who volunteered to participate in a test–retest paradigm which was designed to evaluate the reliability of computer controlled administration of the Peabody Picture Vocabulary Test (PPVT). Each subject was tested on both forms of the PPVT. After each test, the subject was asked to respond to three dichotomous questions (see Table 8.1). Of the 122 responses received for the work–play dichotomy, the percentage of responses was 40% and 60% for work and play respectively. In the relative length dichotomy, 54% were "long" while 46% of the 133 responses were "short." For the percentage of responses to the easy–hard question, 19% of the responses included both "easy" and "hard." Of those responses that were in the suggested dichotomy, the percentage of responses were 83% and 17%, respectively.

Although Elwood and Clark reported the attrition of six subjects (one who refused to complete the second test and five others who were excluded because their scores on at least one form were below the extrapolated norms listed in the PPVT manual), they did not elaborate on subject characteristics. Subsequent research should investigate the characteristics of subjects lost from the pool to provide information about individuals who are not candidates for computerized assessment.

Another measure of interest in the Elwood and Clark study is the number of subjects who requested help (pushed the "help" button to obtain assistance). This measure was important because there was no examiner present to answer questions and to reassure the child. The authors report that during the first testing session, 62% of the subjects requested help. During the second session, only 27% sought help.

Griest et al. (1973) measured the reactions of 22 suicidal clients and 43 non-suicidal clients by asking them to state the degree of agreement on six different items. An analysis of client responses indicated no significant differences in (a) the degree to which the clients liked the interview; (b) felt comfortable; (c) felt they got their ideas and feelings across; (d) felt they had been asked the right questions and understood the questions. Of interest is the finding that 52% of the suicidal clients interviewed in-

Table 8.1. Client Reactions to Computerized Assessment

Author	Measures of client reaction and subject variables
1. Gedye & Miller (1969)	Several geriatric patients who refused testing by conventional methods did not object to automated testing.
2. Hedl et al. (1983)	Measures of state anxiety were taken before and after each testing condition using the A-Trait scale State-Trait Anxiety Inventory (STAI). Examples of items include, "I am tense", "I feel ill at ease". In addition, attitudes were measured via a scale modeled after the semantic differential. Finally, prior to and after the computer administered test, subjects completed a checklist specific to their attitudes about the computer.
3. Griest et al. (1973)	Clients were asked to state degree of agreement (five point scale ranging from "not at all" to "extremely") on six different items. In addition, patients were asked who they would rather give information of a private or a personal nature. The choices were a computer or the clinician.
4. Elwood & Clark (1978)	Clients were asked dichotomous questions, i.e., Was testing more like work than play? Was testing long or short? Easy or hard?
5. Lucas (1977)	Clients were given two questionnaires to complete relating to their perceptions of the interview; one "Thurstone" type scale based on attitude scales, and a semantic differential.
6. Katz & Dalby (1981)	Clients were asked which format they preferred (manual or automated).
7. Skinner & Allen (1983)	Clients were asked to complete a fifteen item semantic differential focusing on three domains of evaluation, i.e., good–bad, potency (weak–strong), and activity (fast–slow). In addition, these authors also administered two WAIS subtests, an anxiety scale and a denial scale to assess client characteristics.

dicated that they would rather give information of a private or personal nature to a computer than to a "doctor." This differed from the non-suicidal group (though not significantly) of which 27% indicated that they would prefer a computer. The final point of interest in the Griest et al. study is that the authors report that clients who exceeded 1½ hours in the completion of the interview demonstrated psychomotor retardation or marked ambivalence about the questions. However, all clients who took the interview completed it.

In an attempt to make evaluation of client attitudes toward computer-administered interviews more objective, Lucas (1977) employed two scales of measurement of client attitudes: a 22-item "Thurstone" attitude measure and a Semantic Differential Scale. After completing a computer-administered medical interview, 75 subjects were given the two questionnaires, asked to complete them at home and return them by mail. The return rate was 89%. Of the individuals who returned the questionnaire, 82% had favorable attitudes toward the computer. In addition, 49% rated the computerized medical interview more favorably than physician-conducted interviews. Additional findings indicated that males perceived the computerized interview more favorably than females. The findings indicated that younger individuals and manual workers perceived the computer more favorably than did older individuals and non-manual workers.

More recently, Skinner and Allen (1983) compared client perception of clients who were randomly assigned to one of three interview formats: computer, face-to-face, and self-report via a 15-item semantic differential that had a 5-point scale. In addition, the authors examined the relationship of client characteristics to client preferences. This was accomplished via administration of a variety of assessment devices (WAIS Vocabulary and Digit Symbols subscales, a denial scale, and a state anxiety scale) to each subject prior to assigning experimental condition. Although the inclusion of these additional assessments demonstrate an improvement over previous measures of client reaction, the results may be confounded by the fact that all of the subjects experienced face-to-face assessment before exposure to their designated interview format.

The result of the "ratings of assessment" indicated that clients generally found the computerized interview to be more interesting and relaxing than the face-to-face and self-report formats. The authors interpret this finding to be indicative of favorable acceptance. In addition, the computerized interview rated higher on activity items, but was perceived as less favorable on the cold–friendly axis. The computerized interview appealed most to clients with good visual–motor performance skills and least to better-educated clients who scored higher on the denial scales. Self report was preferred by clients who were older, defensive, and higher on verbal abilities. Face-to-face was more acceptable to females and clients high on denial, but less acceptable to anxious clients whose anxiety level may have been exacerbated by interpersonal contact.

In spite of the fact that different measures were used by Skinner and Allen (1983) and Lucas (1977), two findings are consistent across the studies: Males reported more favorable ratings of the computer assessment than females, and younger subjects reported more favorable ratings than older subjects of the computer assessment. These findings seem to indicate that computer assessment may be more efficacious (or at least better received) for some clients than others. Additional research is needed to examine subject characteristics which might be predictive of optimal testing conditions for a given client. One seemingly obvious variable which has not been included in these studies is the client's past experience with computers.

One final study that compared subjects' state anxiety in the computer to the traditional testing situation is noteworthy in spite of its methodological problems. Hedl et al. (1973) hypothesized that evaluative stress, to the degree that it depends on the interpersonal relationship between the examiner and the examinee, should be reduced in a computer-administered test condition. In a test of this hypothesis, 48 college students were randomly assigned to one of three groups which differed only in the order of the presentation of three intelligence tests—the Weschler Adult Intelligence Test (WAIS), the Slosson Intelligence Test (SIT), and the SIT administered via computer. Measures of state anxiety and an attitude scale modeled after the semantic differential were administered before and after each test administration. Prior to receiving the computerized version of the SIT, subjects were asked to complete a brief attitude scale which required them to respond by anticipating their reactions to the computerized assessment. Following testing, the scale was readministered to assess actual reactions to computer testing.

The results indicated that the STA1 A-state scores were higher in the computer testing situation when compared to the two conventional examiner-administered test situations. Additional analyses indicate that attitudes toward computer testing were less favorable than face-to-face testing in all three groups.

Hedl and his associates report that student comments about the experiment indicate that procedural variables, such as clarity of instructions and lack of familiarity with the computer terminal, may have strongly influenced affective reactions. An additional problem encountered with the computer-administered test was that the test was not terminated when the student reached his ceiling (10 consecutive incorrect responses). As a result, the students received the entire set of remaining test items. The authors suggest that this might have contributed to the evaluative stress manifested by the students.

Issues Involved in Computerized Testing

A major problem with respect to psychological testing is the trend to transform traditional psychological tests into a computerized format. Logically, this strategy makes sense in that certain traditional psychological tests are commonly used in clinical practice, have demonstrated reliability and validity, provide normative data which facilitates computerized scoring, and have explicit rules for interpretation.

However, traditional assessment procedures have been criticized for their focus on the identification of underlying personality traits as a means for predicting behavior and their lack of utility in the design of treatment. Kanfer and Saslow (1969), and Goldfried and Kent (1972) provide an excellent review of this position. Space (1981), in reviewing the criticisms of computer-aided assessment noted: "Computerized approaches describe an individual as a point on a continuum in comparison with the rest of the population, but they are not geared to regularities and patterns unique to that single individual. Thus, the clinically more important idiographic information is lost in favor of nomothetic information" (p. 599).

Some authors have raised questions about whether the computer versions of standardized tests are in reality, testing the same abilities. Duthrie (1984), for example, has suggested that the client's response set (as defined by their preconceived attitudes to the computer) may contaminate test results. Further, although there appears to be little difference in the completion of a paper-and-pencil task and a task performed at a computer terminal, Duthrie hypothesized that in fact, different cognitive processes are required for the completion of the two tasks. He therefore concluded that computerized versions of currently used psychological tests may not be valid. One final point made by Duthrie is noteworthy: As indicated earlier, one of the major advantages of computer-administered tests was the fact that standardized test presentation was guaranteed. However, Duthrie pointed out that computer-administered assessment lacks a standard format; for example, CRTs and keyboards are not standardized. They differ on a number of dimensions including the physical characteristic (size, color), the number of characters that are displayed across the screen (ranging from 40 to 80), the color of the characters, the keyboard size, layout, and tactile cues. This lack of standardization has the potential to compromise the validity of a computer-administered test.

REFERENCES

Byers, A. P. (1981). Psychological evaluation by means of an on-line computer. *Behavior Research Methods and Instrumentation, 4,* 585–587.
Duthrie, B. (1984). A critical examination of computer-administered psychological

tests. In M. D. Schwartz (Ed.), *Using computers in clinical practice: Psychotherapy and mental health applications* (pp. 135–139). New York: Haworth Press.

Elwood, D. L., & Clark, C. L. (1978). Computer administration of Peabody Picture Vocabulary Test to young children. *Behavior Research Methods and Instrumentation, 10,* 43–46.

Gedye, J. L., & Miller, E. (1969). The automation of psychological assessment. *International Journal of Man-Machine Studies, 1,* 237–262.

Goldfried, M. R., & Kent, R. N. (1972). Traditional vs. behavioral personality assessment: A comparison of methodological & theoretical assumptions. *Psychological Bulletin, 1972, 77,* 409–420.

Greist, J. H., Gustafson, D. H., Strauss, F. F., Rowse, G. L., Langren, T. P., & Chiles, J. A. (1973). A computer interview for suicide risk prevention. *American Journal of Psychiatry, 130,* 1327–1332.

Hedl, J. J., O'Neil, H. F., & Hansen, D. H. (1973). Affective reactions toward computer based intelligence testing. *Journal of Consulting and Clinical Psychology, 40,* 217–222.

Johnson, J. H. (1984). An overview of computerized testing. In M. D. Schwartz (Ed.), *Using computers in clinical practice: Psychotherapy and mental health applications* (pp. 131–133). New York: Haworth Press.

Johnson, J. H., Gianetti, R. A., & Williams, T. A. (1975). Real time psychological assessment and evaluation of psychiatric patients. *Behavior Research Methods and Instrumentation, 7,* 199–200.

Johnson, J. H., & Williams, T. A. (1975). The use of on-line computer technology in a mental health admitting system. *American Psychologist, 30,* 388–390.

Kanfer, F. H., & Saslow, G. (1969). Behavioral diagnosis. In C. M. Franks (Ed.), *Behavior therapy: Appraisal and status* (pp. 417–444). New York: McGraw-Hill.

Katz, L., & Dalby, J. T. (1981). Computer and manual administration of the Eysenk Personality Inventory. *Journal of Clinical Psychology, 37,* 586–588.

Lucas, R. W. (1977). A study of patient's attitudes to computer interrogation. *International Journal of Man Machine Studies, 9,* 69–86.

Roid, G. H., & Gorsuch, R. L. (1984). Development and clinical use of test-interpretive programs on microcomputers. In M. D. Schwartz (Ed.), *Using computers in clinical practice: Psychotherapy and mental health applications* (pp. 141–149). New York: Haworth Press.

Skinner, H. A., & Allen, B. A. (1983). Does the computer make a difference? Computerized vs. face to face self-report assessment of alcohol, drug, and tobacco use. *Journal of Consulting and Clinical Psychology, 51,* 267–275.

Space, L. (1981). The computer as psychometrician. *Behavior Research Methods and Instrumentation, 13,* 595–606.

Spitzer, R. L., & Endicott, J. (1969). Diagnosis II: Further developments in a computer program for psychiatric diagnosis. *American Journal of Psychiatry, 125,* (Supplement), 12–21.

Chapter 9
Me Gereo, Ergo Sum

As the title of this chapter implies (the translation is "I behave, therefore I am," for those who have not had the benefit of attending a high school in which Latin was a required language), there is a particular orientation in our field that assumes that behavior is the most important unit of analysis. Although it certainly has many associated terms, "the behavioral approach" is characterized by a strong, although not exclusionary, focus on current events in the individual's environment and great care is taken to specify and quantify behaviors, interactions, and setting stimuli. The applied practice of the behavioral approach is often technically difficult because the procedures for collection and analysis of such specific behavior information are complex and often time consuming. In this regard, the interface of computer technology with the behavioral approach is a very exciting and appropriate one. Specifically, computer technology can have positive impact in the areas of behavior observation and behavior analysis.

BEHAVIOR OBSERVATION

There is an extensive and long-standing literature concerning the methodology of behavior observation. Typically, behavior observation involves a paper-and-pencil system to record observations of an individual or individuals over a short fixed period of time. For example, an individual is observed for 10 seconds, the information is recorded in a numbered grid, and the process repeated for a predetermined duration. Such a system seeks to impose a time base upon the flow of behavior in order to provide some means for quantification and temporal analysis, and at a practical level, the system seeks to impose a marker that can be used for reliability assessment. There are many variations on this methodology, but one chooses a specific set of target behaviors to observe and then records information as to their presence or absence, their duration or latency, their sequence, or whatever format is appropriate for both the behaviors and questions under study. Such observation systems provide a wealth of important information applicable both within the research as well as the clinical setting. However, such systems are noted for their cumbersome nature and are plagued with numerous pragmatic problems, not the least of which is having the observers adhere to a strict time base and to synchronize the observations of multiple observers.

If one uses the medium of video tape, many of these problems can be significantly reduced. One can start and stop tapes, return to a segment that was missed while one was in the process of picking up a shattered stop watch that had been dropped, and so forth. The task of synchronization and adhering to a time base still remains, as do the simple mechanics of counting frequency, converting to percentage of occurrence, and computing reliability. There is significant literature to suggest that such problems are not simply speculative, but rather can be significant methodological problems.

The microcomputer provides an interesting alternative. The basic requirement for such a system is a keyboard, a method of moderate data storage (preferably a disk drive), a printer, and an internal clock for the computer. These requirements are easily met by most microcomputer systems. One then has the task of programming the computer to serve as an aid for observation. While I would not underestimate the complexity of such a task, a simple observation program is within the range of ability of a somewhat experienced user, given some time and effort. Also, appearing at this time are advertisements for specific software for this type of application.

The following simple program in BASIC for the Apple IIe could be used to collect observational data. The keyboard is used by placing small, stick-on labels over certain keys and writing a specific behavior or event on each. For our purposes we will use the first nine numerals on the keyboard, that is, numbers 1, 2, 3, 4, 5, etc. The basic structure for collection is simply to continuously scan the keyboard. When a key is pressed, the elapsed time from the clock is recorded, this value is stored in an array, and finally the program returns to scanning the keyboard. This process is continued until a signal from the keyboard indicates to stop. In this particular case the "0" key will indicate stop.

PROGRAM	COMMENTS
10 DIM PRS$(500),TM$(500)	establish data array for variables
20 D$=CHR$ (4)	set variable for format command
100 FOR I=1 TO 500	scan up to 500 entries
110 GET A1$	read the keyboard
120 IF A1$="0" THEN NE=I: GOTO 160	If key=0 then abort
130 GOSUB 1000	get time
140 PRS$ (I)=A1$:TM$(I)=A$	store current variables in the array
150 NEXT I	continue the loop

```
160 PR# 1                            turn printer on
170 FOR I=1 TO NE                    scan from 1st to last element
180 PRINT PRS$(I);TM$(I)             print data for each cell of the array
190 NEXT I                           continue the loop
200 PR# 0                            turn printer off
210 END                              stop the program
1000 ROM Read internal clock         subroutine to read clock
1010 PRINT : PRINT D$;"PR#4":         this is specific to clock installed
     PRINT D$;"IN#4"
1020 INPUT "%";A$                     A$=current time
1030 PRINT D$;"PR#0": PRINT D$;       return to normal mode
     "IN#0"
1040 RETURN                          return to main program
```

This sample print-out from the program indicates the letter pressed and the time at which it occurred.

5	MON JAN 14	4:10:37 PM
1	MON JAN 14	4:10:39 PM
4	MON JAN 14	4:10:44 PM
9	MON JAN 14	4:10:44 PM
8	MON JAN 14	4:10:50 PM
3	MON JAN 14	4:10:52 PM
5	MON JAN 14	4:10:55 PM
2	MON JAN 14	4:10:58 PM

This program is, of course, minimally functional as it simply prints a table of values. However, given this information the next step is to construct an analysis program. If one wished to analyze latency between specific behaviors, one would scan this array of data, find the first instance of the target behavior and note the time, scan further to find the next instance, subtract the first time from the current time and store the difference in another array. Thus, one would build up a series of arrays with each containing specific information, whether it be frequency, latency, duration, sequence, and so on. Even though the conceptualization of such programs as to the various functions and analysis to be performed is not complex, the programming can be quite sophisticated and is not an easy task for the novice. Applications such as this are good examples of where the purchase of commercial programs or where enlisting the aid of a professional programmer is wise. Development time of software for such purposes can be extensive and can detract from valuable research time. On the other hand, if one is part of a group in which there are some individuals with moderate programming skills, then this type task is not unrealistic and could be pursued with a reasonable expectation of success.

I use three separate computer systems in my work. The first is a standard microcomputer system that has been adapted to accommodate 32 separate key inputs from a customized keyboard. This keyboard was designed for ease of use and to fit the left and right hand comfortably. It is used primarily for scoring video tapes, permitting high-speed processing of the data collected, and storing each session on disk files. This permits the rapid calculation of various measures of reliability among different observers by comparing sessions that are stored on the disk, and saves enumerable hours in calculation time. Therefore, complex analyses can be routinely performed that were previously prohibitive or unfeasible. Also, the computer greatly speeds up the training process, as reliability estimates can be computed by a variety of methods quickly and more precisely than by manual means.

Such a system, however, does have a drawback in that it is large and not transportable, which makes it only suitable for videotape analysis. To meet the need of in vivo observation, we have constructed two other systems. The first is based upon the Radio Shack PC2 pocket computer. This device, with its associated printer, measures only 12" by 4" by 2" high. It has a built-in internal clock and is ideal because it is small and portable. It runs on internal batteries so no external power supply is required. However, because of limited memory size, the software used is able to record only six behaviors at a time in a mutually exclusive format. As currently used, the system is designed to operate for 30 minutes and then print an analysis of the observations. Most often, the unit is placed on a teacher's desk in a classroom and the key corresponding to one of six target behaviors is depressed. At the end of 30 minutes, a table is printed out with the sequence of behaviors and associated times of occurrence, a frequency analysis for all behaviors, and a graph indicating their relative distribution. Further, a probability table is printed that indicates the frequency with which each behavior is associated with each other behavior within a 10-second "window." Thus, this device serves well for collecting preliminary information in a manner that does not unduly tax the user. These units can be reproduced for approximately $400 and because the calculations are performed immediately, they are able to provide immediate feedback to the individuals present.

A second system negates some of the limitations associated with the small unit. For general purpose usage that combines portability, ease of use, and that allows collection of many of behaviors and events, Epson's HX-20 computer was chosen. This device has a full-sized keyboard, which reduces entry error associated with the smaller "pocket-sized" microcomputers, and is about the size of a loose leaf notebook. It also has a built-in clock, a micro-cassette drive for storing information on miniature cassettes and a built-in printer. Thus, it is completely self-contained and portable.

FIGURE 9.1. A research assistant using a small portable computer to record child interactions from a video-taped segment. The small paper circles taped onto the keys are labeled with the specific target behavior that the key represents.

The software we developed allows one to collect up to 26 individual behaviors or events and to do this either in the interval mode where a time base is set, such as 5 seconds, 10 seconds, 15 seconds, or in an event mode in which one depresses the appropriate key for the duration of the behavior or event. This microcomputer has a substantial memory and thus allows for relatively long recording sessions, even for high-frequency behavior. The data analysis is also quite complex given the speed and memory capabilities of this microcomputer. The built-in printer utilizes 2″-wide paper that, although somewhat restrictive, is adequate for in vivo utilization. Figure 9.2 is an example of parts of the print-out that are obtained from an interval-sampling session.

The first section indicates basic information about the start and stop time of the sampling period, the titles given to identify the segment, and the total elapsed time. Also indicated is the bin or interval size and the total

FIGURE 9.2. A sample print-out of the data analysis from the observations recorded with the computer in Figure 9.1. The computer prints on an internal small printer that uses 2″-wide paper, resulting in this type of format.

number of intervals scored. The strip chart corresponds to the 26 letters of the alphabet on the keyboard and presents an easy format for visual inspection of the data. The next section is an example of the analysis that is printed for each behavior recorded. In this example, for the letter "Q," used to indicate a particular behavior, the frequency, rate per minute, and percentage of distribution is analyzed, as is the duration of episodes or "bouts" of behavior. Further, interresponse times are analyzed in an analogous fashion. Next, the probability tables are printed, in this case indicating the frequency of occurrence within the same interval and also one interval past the target behavior. The user can set this "window" for any duration so that one may examine the relationship between the occurrence of a particular behavior and the subsequent occurrence of others. This would be useful, for example, in analyzing the effects of a group leader's verbal prompting on the subsequent verbal behavior of members of the group. By using different windows to analyze the same data, one can determine empirically the type of temporal relationship that exists.

The data analyses are so extensive and complex that use of the microcomputer is extremely beneficial. These analyses are cumbersome if done manually, and they take time that could be better spent in either data collection or interpretation. To further assist in this process, such small, portable microcomputers can be linked to larger and more powerful systems. In my own laboratory, the HX-20 is connected via a cable to an Apple computer so that data collected in the field and stored on cassette tape is transferred to the Apple to be stored on disk. This permits easy categorization and filing of sessions and also permits rapid retrieval and high-speed analysis. Use of such an integrated system permits very good levels of efficiency with respect to utilizing research assistants and observers. Further, one need make no trade-offs during pilot phases of either research or clinical programs with respect to data collection and analysis, as the computer automatically performs the typically tedious and error-prone task of complex data analysis.

BEHAVIORAL ASSESSMENT

Related to behavior observation and behavior analysis is the more general process of behavioral assessment. It is a process of gathering specific information concerning an individual's history, current behavior and, in the broad sense of the term, their environment. Interestingly, behavioral assessment is a term often used in the clinical literature, but it is rarely defined precisely nor are examples usually given. This is perhaps because it is a process, and therefore dynamically related to each individual. Nevertheless, there are some general guidelines. For the present example, which assumes the client is a child, there are a number of specific areas that must be addressed. Thus, the Table 9.1 would represent the basic elements of a behavioral assessment.

An inspection of Table 9.1 indicates that a diverse set of information is to be collected. Herein lies, I believe, one of the major difficulties with the behavioral assessment: it does not lend itself to an easily quantified structure. It relies very heavily upon the interpretation of the clinician and upon sophisticated skills in organization of information. Since in most cases, norms are not available or are not appropriate, a behavioral assessment also does not lend itself well to the type of standardized review found for many traditionally, intellectual and personality assessment devices.

One aid that can be very powerful is the free-form data base. This was discussed in chapter 7, and in the context of the review of the various data bases, I had stated that these free-form type data bases should not be the initial choice of the user. The primary reason for this is that these data bases place constraints upon the user in terms of attempting to organize the information as it is entered, because there is little provision for formatted output. With specific reference to behavioral assessment however, there can be an advantage to using a free-form data base. If, as one gathers information for the behavioral assessment and begins to form tentative hypotheses, and if the information entered into the data base is consistent with respect to using key words, then the process will be functional. For instance, in reviewing family interactions and investigating potential reinforcers, an item might be entered as "trips to the miniature golf course with Dad appear to be a reinforcer." By using such key words as "reinforcer" and by identifying family members as one proceeds through the information-gathering steps of the outline, one could for instance, request a list of reinforcers from the data base. In like manner, one could select activities with Dad that are reinforcers and so on and so forth. Because a well-conducted behavioral assessment does indeed have a series of steps associated with it and because these steps involve investigation of specific behavior patterns and variables, this free-form type of data base can be useful for making "give me everything about _____" type requests.

Of course, one can perform the same task by hand readily by using a paper-and-pencil outline system. However, the utility of the computer arises as the complexity of the analysis increases. For instance, if one were conducting a behavioral assessment with a family where there are many complex interactions among numerous family members, then this type of data-base assistance can be beneficial. It would be important to note, however, that such utilization of the computer would not be a replacement for traditional notes and summaries, but rather it is an adjunct to quickly ascertain possible relationships among the information. In the future, as data bases become more sophisticated and flexible, it may be possible to combine the free-form data base with structured output so that

Table 9.1. Elements of a Behavior Analysis

I. Historical Analysis
  A. Interview
    1. Developmental history
    2. Social history
    3. Medical history
    4. Family/living environment history
  B. Review existing records
  C. Behavior change history
    1. Specific behaviors
    2. Specific procedures
    3. Behavior change agent characteristics
    4. Degree of success
    5. Unplanned positive effects
    6. Unplanned negative effects
    7. Permanence
    8. Generalization

II. Behavior Parameters
  A. Behavior excesses
    1. Frequency
    2. Intensity
    3. Duration
    4. Latency
    5. Stimulus control
    6. Collateral behaviors
    7. Currently occurring positive consequences
    8. Currently occurring negative consequences
    9. Hypothesized controlling variables
    10. Observed vs. acceptable omission
  B. Behavior deficits
    1. Frequency
    2. Intensity
    3. Duration
    4. Latency
    5. Stimulus control
    6. Collateral behaviors
    7. Currently occurring positive consequences
    8. Currently occurring negative consequences
    9. Hypothesized motivational variables
    10. Observed vs. required emission
    11. Missing behavior repertoire components
  C. Behavior assets
    1. Relation to behavior excesses and deficits
    2. Relative strength
    3. Degree of stimulus control
    4. Degree to which:
      a. age appropriate
      b. functional
      c. spontaneous vs. elicited
        1. degree of prompting required
        2. type of prompting required

Table 9.1. *continued*

D. Behavior constraints
  1. Situational opportunity
  2. Living environment expectations (norms/values)
  3. Physical
  4. Sensory
  5. Perceptual
  6. Neurological
  7. Medication

III. Contingency Survey
  A. Behavior accelerators available
    1. Primary
    2. Tangible
    3. Social
    4. Symbolic
  B. Behavior decelerators available
    1. Primary
    2. Tangible
    3. Social
    4. Symbolic

IV. Ecological Analysis
  A. Will demands upon individual increase/decrease?
  B. Will demands upon significant others increase/decrease?
  C. Will significant others benefit if change occurs?
  D. Who supports anticipated treatment program?
  E. Who will not support anticipated treatment program?
  F. Does significant disagreement exist concerning goals and/or treatment methodology?
  G. Are sufficient resources available to implement treatment?
    1. Short-term
    2. Long-term
    3. For generalization
    4. For continuing consultation/support
  H. Are others who are involved with the individual also in need of therapeutic/support services?
  I. What is the individual's status and relationship with other members of the family/living unit.

V. Ethical Concerns (Procedural safeguards)
  A. Does individual indicate desire for change?
  B. Do the parents/guardians indicate desire for change?
  C. Is there an objective advocate?
  D. Is there a consensus for change?
  E. Can the individual give consent?
  F. Can the individual assist in developing the treatment program?
  G. Can the parents/guardians assist in developing in treatment program?
  H. Have issues of community standards and transition been considered?
  I. Has peer review been sought?
  J. Is there support for treatment approach in the professional literature?

more integrative reports could be generated. At this time, however, such data bases are not available and therefore, some degree of compromise occurs with respect to the efficiency of any particular data base.

Since behavioral assessment is an ongoing process, the free-form data base can also be appropriately used for therapy notes. The use of such a system for therapy notes would not be restricted to an individual applying a behavioral approach. It is often useful to be able to interrogate the computer to ask a question such as "when did the client make reference to work related stress?" One could find such information by reviewing hand-written reports and notes, or if one had routinely entered such information into the computer, then retrieval would be a very fast and easy process. However, the caution here again is that the format of entry into the computer would have to include not only the reference of stress at work, but also the date of the session. In the absence of placing such markers into the record, all that could be retrieved was the statement concerning stress at work and not its relation to other events or time.

The potential for storing and retrieving on-going client records and assessment information with a computer data base is very high. It is not an easy application however, and the current software does not fully lend itself to this application. Caution is urged in pursuing this route. It is best avoided by the novice. However, it also holds great promise for the clinician as a system to enhance accuracy and comprehensiveness of information-gathering and analysis for the decision-making process.

Chapter 10
Data Analysis

STATISTICAL ANALYSIS

Statistical analysis of data, whether it be for clinical, administrative, or research purposes, is a task that many psychologists must perform routinely. The sophistication required can range from simple, descriptive statistics to multivariate analysis. As mentioned in the chapter on telecommunications, most of us are familiar with such analyses, whether it be through the use of key-punch data or direct entry on a terminal to a large, mainframe computer. Again as described in the chapter on telecommunications, it is reasonable and convenient to use the microcomputer as an extension of the large, mainframe computer and to use its extensive memory and storage capacity as well as its sophisticated analysis program.

However, as the demands from individuals who do not have access to such computer facilities for sophisticated data analysis have grown, more and more sophisticated software programs designed to run on microcomputers that emulate many of the important characteristics associated with mainframe data analysis have begun to appear. Starting simply, however, an excellent candidate for one's first excursion into the process of writing one's own program is descriptive statistics. There are numerous basic programming books available for a variety of computer languages that use simple statistical analysis examples as the method for teaching programming. As the formulas we use for descriptive statistics are relatively simple, this mechanism for learning programming is relatively painless and has a productive outcome.

As one increases the complexity of analyses desired, it becomes much more complex to create the program. The increase in complexity in the formulas required to complete the analyses is not the element of difficulty, but rather one must be concerned with data storage, the construction of data matrices, and routines that allow for editing the data, compensating for missing data points, transformation functions, and so on. Such programs incorporate elements of a data base for data management as well as for the statistical analyses.

It is not uncommon for many retail stores to have access to public domain software, which are software programs that have been written by individuals who allow these programs to be copied and used free of charge by anyone who is interested. There is a wide array of statistical analysis programs among the public domain software, although one should check any such programs by performing the calculations manually at least once or twice to ascertain accuracy. Because these are public domain programs, there is no guarantee of accuracy. One is simply benefiting from the time and effort that someone else has devoted in learning to use their microcomputer for various tasks. Such programs are fine for the individual who performs only occasional analyses and wishes to gain some increment of speed over using a hand calculator. However, if frequent and extensive statistical analysis is to be used for administrative and/or research purposes, then one would be well advised to investigate the powerful data analysis systems currently available. Many of these packages will closely emulate the options available on a mainframe computer, including multivariate analysis. However, since there is no standardization among such programs, it is important to realize that each will be slightly different and will tend to emphasize or deemphasize certain procedures. Therefore, as discussed in the section on assessment and diagnosis, it is very important that one obtain the user's manual for the statistic software as well as sample print-outs and a list of features. Some of these packages can be rather expensive ranging from $100 to $2,000. In many cases, the increased cost reflects capabilities, ease of use and data manipulation, and speed of execution. Certainly one should not expect to emulate the speed of the mainframe computer, but if one were to examine the total time of interaction with the computer from data entry to printed results, in many cases the microcomputer system will outperform the mainframe if the user has access to it at any time desired and without restrictions.

Although many sophisticated microcomputer statistical programs appear to have a wide range of desirable functions, be sure to ascertain the limit imposed concerning number of variables and number of cases that can be analyzed. This is particularly important if one is conducting large-group, repeated measures design. Most users of mainframe computers have been "spoiled" by virtually unlimited storage capabilities on these large computers. The microcomputer does place very clear constraints upon memory utilization in particular and I cannot underscore strongly enough that the user must be cautious in approaching a statistical analysis program for the microcomputer. In my own work, I have found one of the moderately priced packages to be exceptionally useful, and I have found that I can have even one of my most noncomputer-oriented students performing complex analyses of their data within an hour of opening the user's manual and running the program. Well-designed, statistical analysis programs are quite user-friendly and they have little resemblance to the often frustrating statistical analysis programs one finds on a large mainframe computer. The primary reason for this is that on the micro-computer, these programs are interactive and menu-driven so that ease of operation is maximized.

In a related area, there are now software programs that assist in the process of teaching statistics. I can vividly remember as an undergraduate at the State University of New York at Stony Brook being involved in one of the first computer-assisted instruction programs for teaching statistics to psychology majors. We would enter a large, dimly lit soundproof room in the bowels of one of the buildings on campus and engage in rather fascinating interactions with the computer as it vainly, at least in my case, tried to make learning statistics a nonaversive event. Given the novelty of this approach at the time, I am perhaps making too negative an evaluation, as most of my classmates and myself were more interested in simply the reactions of the computer to our input rather than in the subject matter per se. Most of us could not resist the rather childish impulse to see how the computer would react to the use of "colorful" language. We were quite surprised to see that, in fact, the computer had a larger repertoire of such language than we did, thanks to the seasoned graduate students who assisted in the programming and who were adept at predicting the behavior of undergraduates.

Distinctly different from the software designed for analysis and instruction in statistics, is software designed to assist the user in determining what statistical analysis to perform and, more importantly, to assist in the choice of design. One such program I have had the opportunity to review that will be released shortly is a marvelous example of what is sometimes termed an *expert* system. As was discussed in chapter 8, software that functions essentially as a colleague to prompt and help organize information can be quite beneficial. In this particular case, the software program asks for information concerning the research design and it provides feedback to the user as to appropriate choices and strategy. Interacting with such programs is always fascinating as again, it appears that one is dealing with an "intelligence." One of our resident statistical experts tested the program by utilizing the masters theses of several students in our department to see if, in fact, the program would yield the same results as obtained by the traditional process of a student and committee hashing out and finally agreeing upon a design. The program performed very well in this test. Such programs are interesting from a practical point of view, and are an indication of the continuing evolution of software programs.

VISUAL ANALYSIS

The task of converting numerical information into graphs to increase clarity of presentation is an activity associated with virtually all areas of psychology and is common practice in other fields as well. The production of graphs can be beneficial, whether one is looking at trends in departmental budgets, the percentage of homework assignments completed by clients in therapy, subject response patterns in an experiment, or the construction of single-subject graphs to assist in decision making. At one level, the requirement for the computer seems to be quite simple. A data array holds the necessary numerical information and the computer takes this information and plots it on a coordinate system on the CRT. Given this display on the CRT, it is usually easy to have this information printed on a dot matrix printer.

Many commercials for microcomputers illustrate the graphics ability of these devices. The graphs can be produced in a variety of resolutions and in monochrome or color. However, there are some cautions that must be raised. Although the color displays look impressive and appear to function well in presenting data, the difficulty is that most printers print the image in black and white, not in color. Therefore, there is no significant advantage in constructing graphs in color, as they cannot be easily transmitted via paper copy. Printers that will print in color as well as X-Y plotters that use color inks are certainly available and can be considered. It is essential, however, that the user determine that the computer hardware, the software, and the color printing devices are compatible. In most cases the construction of compatible systems can be a difficult task. Even if an appropriate color printer or plotter is used, most copiers—assuming the graphs are to be distributed to a number of individuals—produce black and white copies.

In general, computer software for the production of graphs is not geared toward the needs of the behavioral scientist. It is not uncommon to find limitations such as the restriction of only plotting either 12 or 31 points on the X axis. This corresponds to 12 months per year or the number of days in the longest month. This type of format is fine for business applications, but has little relevance for many clinical applications. In like manner, many software programs are geared more toward the production of bar charts or pie charts, which again are useful for many administrative or accounting procedures but are of limited relevance for clinical purposes.

Thus, the impediment is typically the software and not the hardware. Paradoxically, the basic software is quite simple. As an example, on most microcomputers if one wishes to draw a line, a command typically of the format "plot x,y to x1,y1" is used. Depending upon the resolution of the screen, one has a coordinate system that usually starts at the top left corner of the screen indicating coordinates 0,0. Using this system it is thus easy to connect any two points and to construct appropriate grids for scaling the data. Once this grid has been established on the screen, plotting the data is done by using the value in the data matrix as the Y coordinates and stepping one increment for each point in the matrix along the X axis. Table 10.1 is an example of a simple program written in BASIC for the Apple IIe computer that will plot data on the screen. Figure 10.1 displays the result that occurs when the program is run.

Table 10.1 is, of course, a working example rather than a finished program. In fact, the program I use is many times larger and more complex and sophisticated than this example. In addition to plotting the information on the screen, one must also scale the data, put in appropriate headings, axes labels, and numbers for the axes gradations. A system is also required to store and retrieve data to a disk file and to permit an easy method of entering and then editing the data to be used. The full program, which took a great deal of time to write, produced the results seen in Figure 10.2.

It is almost certain that a program to produce graphs will not perform the functions that you require. Therefore, it is very important to obtain sample output of software you are considering and carefully investigate what restrictions are on its usage. For instance, the relatively common practice of "stacking" graphs to observe interactions between individuals or target behaviors is not a common function in graphing programs, nor is the ability to overlay multiple graphs on the same axes if there are any missing data points among the various curves. As requests for such software continue to increase, thus making the market a profitable one for software developers, more sophisticated graphics programs will appear that will handle the needs of researchers and clinicians. At present however, exercise caution in the selection of such software, or embark on the rather prodigious task of creating your own custom program. Useful software exists, but a careful analysis of your needs and the software's features is a prerequisite to finding the right program.

COST BENEFIT

The use of appropriate software is not necessarily cost-effective for producing graphs. If the task is to produce a graph for publication, presentation at a conference, or for inclusion in an assessment or progress report, then the computer can save significant time and effort. In contrast, if the need is to produce a continuing series of individual graphs for clients or subjects, then the software is not usually cost-effective. In the first example, all the data were available and would be used to produce a graph that, when printed, would be complete. In the second example, data would

Table 10.1. Simple Program Written in BASIC
for the Apple IIe

PROGRAM

```
5      SO=8
10     DIM D(25)
15     HGR
20     HCOLOR=3
30     X0=79:Y0=20
35     X1=279:Y1=120
40     GOSUB 2000
45     GOSUB 2070:GOSUB 3100
50     X=X0
110    FOR I=1 TO 20
120    READ D(I)
130    NEXT I
140    FOR I=1 TO 20
150    I1-I-1
160    D=D(I):D1=D(I+1)
170    HPLOT X+(SO*I1), Y-D TO
       X+(SO*I1)+SO, Y-D1
180    NEXT I
190    INPUT Z$
200    TEXT
210    STOP
2000   REM DRAW GRAPH OUTLINE
2010   HPLOT X0,Y0 TO X1, Y0 TO X1,
       Y1 TO X0, Y1 TO X0,Y0
2020   REM DRAW SCREEN BORDER
2030   HPLOT 0,0 TO 279,0 TO 279,1
       59 TO 0,159 TO 0,0
```

be arriving in a continuous stream and the graph would be continuously updated and reprinted.

Especially in facilities that utilize the behavior analysis approach to habilitative programming such as a facility for the developmentally disabled, it is common to see hundreds of graphs that are produced to allow for assessment of resident progress. This task is burdensome, involves great time and effort, and often results in a multitude of different formats, scaling procedures, levels of accuracy, as well as a wide range of aesthetic appearances. Thus, it is often considered to be a good candidate for computerization, but indeed, it is not. This can be most easily demonstrated by imagining two individuals, each of whom have the task of monitoring and updating 20 different graphs. Each has a large bulletin board on

Table 10.1. *Continued*

PROGRAM

```
2040  RETURN
2050  DATA 10,20,30,40,40,30,40,
      50,60
2060  DATA 60,10,50,10,50,20,40,
      30,30,40,60,0
2070  REM Y AXIS
2080  FOR I = Y1 TO Y0 STEP - 10
2090  S1 = 5
3000  I1 = I1 + 1
3010  IF I1 = 6 THEN S1 = 10
3020  HPLOT X0,I TO X0 - S1,I
3030  NEXT I
3040  RETURN
3100  REM X AXIS
3110  FOR I = X0 TO X1 STEP S0
3120  S1 = 5
3130  I1 = I1 + 1
3140  IF I1 < 10 THEN 6120
3150  S1 = 10
3160  I1 = 0
3170  HPLOT I,Y1 TO I,Y1 + S1
3180  NEXT I
3190  RETURN
```

---

which these graphs are displayed. As the data arrives at the end of each day for updating, the individual using the manual procedure takes a pencil, walks up to each graph, adds the data point, and connects the line. The process of updating requires but a few seconds per graph. In contrast, the individual who is using the computer must first load the appropriate software program, access each file separately for each of the 20 individuals, and add the data into the existing data matrix for each individual. Then, the file must saved to the diskette and this process repeated for all 20 individuals. Clearly, it takes longer to perform this task with the computer than it does manually. Additionally, the person who has performed the task manually has also updated the graphs on the bulletin board. The person utilizing the computer has not. To update the graphs, each must be reprinted. Even with a high-speed dot matrix printer, this process usu-

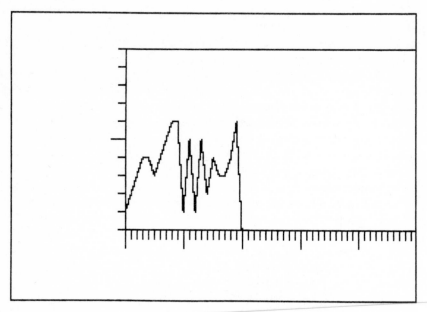

FIGURE 10.1. A display of the output of a simple graphing program.

ally takes several minutes per graph. By adding up this time each day, it is clear that the cost–benefit ratio is in favor of manual updating. One could attenuate this time factor by printing the graphs perhaps only once per week. Of course, this in turn negates the purpose for which the graphs were intended, that of precise daily monitoring.

Thus, while the computer is, in fact, an excellent tool for producing high quality and detailed graphs with great accuracy, it is cumbersome to use if the data is to be continually updated. The user must carefully evaluate the purposes for such graphs and not assume that a computerized system is, in fact, more efficient. In many years of consulting with various individuals and facilities, it is sadly the case that more often than not, the feedback I receive is, ''You're right—it *is* slower to do it by computer,'' after a great deal of time and effort had been spent on attempting to utilize a computerized system.

There are some factors, however, that can change this evaluation. The first is the presence of a very high-speed printer. In this regard, the new laser printers that are now appearing will significantly affect the cost–benefit ratio. These devices will be able to produce a graph in approximately 8 seconds. The quality is extremely good and may serve as an appropriate solution for the problem of printing efficiently, albeit at a high cost.

Even if the problem of printer speed is solved, one still has the problem of the time required to update each individual file. Appropriate attention to details of programming can somewhat attenuate entry time if the program allows for easy flow between functions, and utilizes a mode that is specific to facilitating data input. Nevertheless, perhaps the only significant factor that would influence the decision to utilize a computer system for generating graphs is if the system performs multiple functions in addition to simply producing the graph.

This type of application is described in the chapter on evaluation and can be a significant reason to implement a computerized system. The stated purpose, however, becomes slightly different than producing graphs. The purpose is now one of data management and its utilization for a number of different functions. As an example, if the file structure and record structure are appropriately designed, not only will the sophisticated data management system produce graphs of data contained in individual files, but it can also indicate the status of various habilitative programs for each individual. This is accomplished by incorporating a

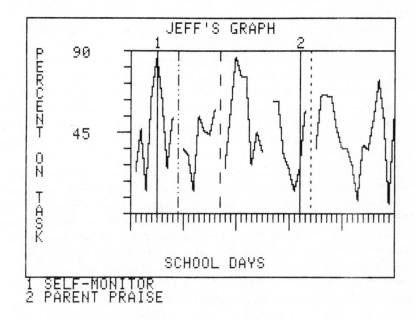

FIGURE 10.2. A more elaborate display from a complex graphing program.

CUMT-D*

function into the software that scans all data files to inspect specific variables. One variable might be set to indicate whether the program was active or inactive, and another variable might indicate what particular area of development the program was designed to address—speech therapy, behavior management, gross motor skills, self-help skills, vocational training, and so on. Other variables would be used to store information concerning the start date of each program as well as its end date, thus allowing for the computation of the length of intervention. Utilizing this information stored in each file, a report format could be designed to produce a list of residents who currently have an active treatment program for behavior management and could specify the target behavior for each of these programs. Such a report could also include the time the program had been in effect. The supervisor might then request a graph for all such programs that have been in existence for more than 60 days. Other reports could focus upon the average duration necessary to accomplish individual habilitative programs or could categorize the areas of intervention to assist in the decision process as to whether or not the individual's total habilitative program is balanced.

As mentioned several times, an excellent criterion for judging the cost benefit of a particular hardware and software system is whether or not information can be processed to serve the needs of multiple functions. Thus, a program to graph data is not necessarily a useful application unless it is used intermittently to produce good-quality graphs at the termination point of data collection. In contrast, if the software is designed to serve a data management function, then, in fact, the time spent in data entry can be justified since important and functional reports are produced in addition to graphs.

The complexity of the data to be analyzed is another factor that can influence the decision to use a microcomputer system for producing graphs. Line graphs and bar charts are relatively simple to produce by hand as well as by computer. Even "overlaying" data sets to produce multiline graphs is straightforward. This type of graph presentation, however, is two dimensional (i.e., plotting the value of a particular variable by one other dimension such as sessions, group size, drug dosage, etc.). This need not be the case, and certainly when conducting exploratory investigations or a complex behavior analysis, it is often useful to conceptualize the process using the interactions of several different variables. As an example, one might be curious about the influence on a particular behavior of a setting-by-time interaction. This type of three-dimensional graph is not as easily produced accurately by hand. It is a small alteration for the computer, and such graphs can be produced with great speed. I have found such three-dimensional graphs, as seen in Figure 10.3, very useful when explaining processes to the lay person or the individual not used to thinking about behavior with such precision.

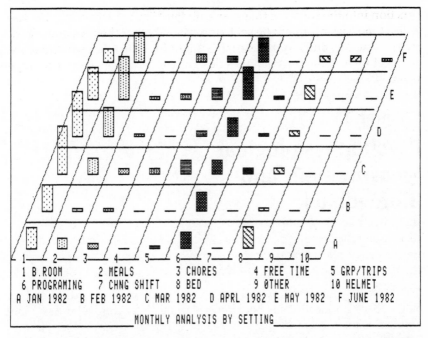

FIGURE 10.3. An example of a three-dimensional display from a complex graphing program.

The graphics capability with most microcomputers is extensive and can be utilized with a wide variety of software programs. It can be an efficient method of data analysis and presentation. The cost benefit is related to user entry time and not the cost of the software itself. Although some programs cost several hundred dollars, this is not expensive for an active user. The specialized plotter and software that I use paid for itself in less than two years due to savings in graphic arts and drafting expenditures. Thus, as mentioned above, carefully analyze the type and amount of information to be processed and how this information will be used and distributed.

Chapter 11

Psychophysiological Measurement and Biofeedback

STRATEGY

The use of a microcomputer in psychophysiological recording and for biofeedback applications is becoming standard. Anyone who has spent hours scoring polygraph charts or teaching others to score charts knows the extreme cost in time and effort and the issues of reliability for such procedures. The microcomputer is ideally suited for such applications as it can (a) simultaneously control the timing and presentation of various stimuli to the client or subject; (b) record the physiological measures of interest; (c) perform on-line analyses of the data for immediate feedback both to the experimenter and to the client in the case of biofeedback; and (d) store the information for future, more complex analysis.

Due to the complexity of the programming, hardware, and various safety considerations with respect to wiring, a microcomputer used for such purposes is a "dedicated" machine. In other words, this is the central task for which it is utilized and it is not typically used for other functions such as word processing, data bases, and so on. This does not have to be the case and, of course, it depends on the particular schedule of activity for the user. If one is contemplating the use of such a system for multiple purposes, then very careful consideration must be given to physical placement of the microcomputer and great care must also be exercised in the wiring of the cables that lead from the microcomputer to the various physiological transducers and then on to the client or subject. In particular, there is a physical limit to the length of cable that can be used to connect the transducers to the computer. This limit is a function of signal strength and interference that is generated over long cable runs. Thus, one must investigate the specific parameters of the equipment to be purchased before planning the physical layout of the facility.

92

HARDWARE

Throughout this book I have attempted to minimize mentioning specifically or endorsing any particular product, as the needs of each individual can drastically affect the appropriate choices. However, in this instance, I can state without hesitation that the best choice of current available microcomputers is the Apple IIe system. For many years, independent manufacturers have been producing sophisticated interfaces for the Apple II line of computers. This level of development is not paralleled in any other microcomputer and thus I believe it is correct to state that at this time, the Apple II system is the standard for use in psychophysiological and biofeedback work on a small-scale basis. There are certainly other, more sophisticated systems, but these are geared more for major research programs and specific procedures that require extremely high speed and many monitoring channels. For the typical research laboratory and the clinical practice that utilizes biofeedback, the Apple IIe system would be the system of choice.

The basic components that are necessary in addition to the microcomputer are a clock/timer interface that is accurate to the millisecond, a digital input/output interface that is used to turn on and off various devices for producing stimuli (such as lights, a tone generator, a tape recorder, a slide projector, etc.), and at least one analog-to-digital converter. Given this basic system, the most efficient method of setting up the complete system is to purchase various physiological transducers from any of several major manufacturers of such devices. One can purchase transducers for heart rate, skin conductance, temperature, and EMG, as well as other more specialized devices. These devices from the major manufacturers are well-designed and reflect appropriate concern for safety issues. Whenever a subject is connected to equipment that uses electrical power, one must be concerned with problems of ground fault and the methods of appropriate subject isolation from the electrical circuitry. In recent years, there has been a proliferation of "hobby" type devices for biofeedback that plug directly into computers such as the Apple IIe. Many of these sell for less than $200 and purport the joys and benefits of biofeedback. I would strongly urge that one not pursue this type of device unless one has some skill and expertise in electronics and electrical safety. The same warning should be given to those who wish to build their own systems from schematics available in different journals and books. Although one pays a premium for the hardware available through the major manufacturers in biofeedback and physiological monitoring equipment, the cost is associated with their expertise and design and manufacturing standards. The typical professional simply does not have these skills, and I believe the cost savings are insignificant compared to the potential dangers. However, I should point out that if one has the necessary skills or can collaborate with an individual skilled in biomedical engineering then substantial monetary savings are possible. But, even in this case, I would urge extreme caution.

SOFTWARE

The software necessary to conduct basic psychophysiological monitoring or biofeedback is not difficult, but it tends to be somewhat lengthy. The basic structure of the software is to enable a free-running clock in the microcomputer to convert two basic analog events into digital information. The first analog event is time. That is, the computer is set to sample the physiological measure at certain time intervals. These intervals are set as a function of the pattern of the particular psychophysiological event under investigation. For instance, with galvanic skin conductance (GSC), sampling the value every half-second is usually sufficient, as this is a relatively slow-reacting measure. Of course, the time base can be set for shorter intervals in the millisecond range. However, if one is attempting to write the software, several other factors must be taken into consideration. One is the computer's processing speed and the execution speed of the programming language. The latter is typically the most important variable. As an example, in utilizing BASIC as a language, one will find that each command may take several milliseconds to execute. A simple way to determine the lower boundary of execution time would be to add a command to read the clock and to store it as a variable into the software section that collects the psychophysiological measure at the start of the subroutine. Then at the end of the subroutine when one cycle of measurement would be completed, again read the clock and store it in a different variable. At that point, print out the difference of the two—that is, subtract the former from the latter. The execution time of the subroutine will be displayed on the screen, and then the limit for resolution will become clear. If one wants to sample a particular event every 200 milliseconds, but this timing analysis indicates that the program requires .5 seconds to execute, the data would be quite useless and interpretation would be impossible.

For this reason, it is often not advisable to begin to write one's own software unless measuring a few slow responding indexes. If one wishes to pursue writing software, then it would be advantageous to purchase an assembler for the program or to learn machine language programming. For either of these two approaches, speed is not a significant problem because the programs will typically execute 10 to 20 times faster than in a language such as BASIC. However, one does trade the relative ease of programming in BASIC with the more complex learning curve associated with machine language programming.

The second analog conversion is that of the psychophysiological measurement itself. Using GSC, as an example, one is attempting to measure a wave form. The analog-to-digital converter simply establishes the range for an electrical signal and segments this range into discrete portions, usually totaling 256 portions. As a side note, such numbers are not arbitrary, and they reflect certain limits of the digital technology. For instance, most analog-to-digital converters used in microcomputer systems are known as 8-bit converters. As we have discussed previously, 8 bits can express a number in a range from 0 to 255, thus the number of segmentations. Analog-to-digital converters are available in different levels of precision, and a 16-bit A-to-D converter would yield much higher levels of resolution. Once this range is established, the analog-to-digital converter samples the wave form, assesses the current instantaneous magnitude and assigns it a value from 0 to 255 based upon which segment the current value falls. Accuracy of measuring the wave form is a function of both the sampling rate (resolution along the x axis) and the resolution of the digitization, which corresponds to increments along the y axis. These factors must be considered for each measurement, as the parameters for heart rate versus GSC versus respiration versus blood pressure are quite different.

COST BENEFIT

Weighing all the factors associated with psychophysiological monitoring, I believe it would be most cost effective to purchase the various components and software from one of the major manufacturers. This way, one has a tool that can be readily and easily utilized and a significant amount of time and effort does not have to be spent on development. Most of the commercial transducers available are quite "intelligent" and perform a fair amount of processing even before the signals are transmitted to the computer. This allows for multiplicity of monitoring. These systems usually have software that can be altered by the user and they also come in "packages" that lend themselves well to biofeedback work and analysis of complex stimuli presentation with corresponding psychophysiological reaction. Most manufacturers will be happy to provide you with names of individuals in your area who have purchased such equipment. A visit to such individuals to discuss their usage and evaluation of the system can be very valuable and can greatly assist in the process of assembling a system for one's own particular needs.

Chapter 12
Children

MOTIVATION

With certain child populations, motivation to participate in treatment programs can be problematic. This can be true whether the program is behaviorally oriented, analytically oriented, or eclectic. Various clinicians use different approaches, terminology and conceptualizations in the attempt to increase motivation. However, the goal of having an attentive and cooperative child client is quite universal. The microcomputer provides an interesting avenue for assisting in this process. Certainly to many children, the microcomputer is perceived simply as a fancy video game and thus, has much of the same attractions. However, unlike video games, which do not have universal appeal among children and which are much too difficult for more severely impaired children to play and enjoy, the microcomputer is far more versatile and thus more useful. The microcomputer can lend itself to a process of assessing the child's interests and preferences and can scale the degree of difficulty or complexity to the individual child.

At first, one can simply purchase software that duplicates many of the popular arcade games. One can achieve a variety of such emulations at relatively low cost. This fact alone would not justify the purchase of a microcomputer system because the purchase of a video game machine would be much less expensive. However, if there is concern about matching the interactions to particular child characteristics, then the choice of a microcomputer is a productive one. Many of the computer-based games are more sophisticated than their video game counterparts and allow for setting of parameters, such as speed and difficulty. Perhaps even more important, it would be wise to obtain software that permits the game to be stopped and the current positions and scores saved to the disk. This permits utilizing the game on a time or response contingent basis, but preserves the flow and the entertaining aspects of it. Certainly, playing an exciting game on the computer and then being interrupted and told that therapy must now start or resume can be a very frustrating experience for a child and can have quite counter productive results.

Also of significance is the range of entertainment software that is available. Clearly, efforts are being made by software vendors to respond to requests for nonviolent entertainment games, to create software that is equally appealing to boys and girls, and to create some especially for female teenagers. In this regard, one can conceptualize the use of microcomputer software as not simply for entertainment, but also as part of the therapeutic process. Games that require cooperative effort and logical thinking can be incorporated as easily as more traditional exercises and activities.

In my own experience, especially in working with learning-disabled children, the microcomputer can be a strong incentive. As part of the children's therapeutic program, we employ a sophisticated token economy that addresses both behavioral and performance goals. The microcomputer is quite effective due to its elaborate nature and we have always been pleased with the impact it has had. Several years ago one of my graduate students, Nancy Ponzetti-Dyer, and I examined the relative effectiveness of access to a microcomputer and our token economy. Interestingly, for many children, the microcomputer was more desirable than aspects of the token economy and soon became their preferred activity. Although initially their access to the microcomputer was simply for the use of various video games, at the end of the project children were earning points in the token economy to purchase time to play with the microcomputer which was running educational software, specifically mathematics activities. Thus, given the versatility of the computer, the growing availability of software that permits individualization, the novelty and carry-over effect of video games, this is an exciting area.

CAUTIONS

Certainly there are concerns in our society about the wisdom of introducing children to computers at early ages and the effect it will have on their social interactions and educational progress. Some of these concerns are well taken and others, I believe, are simply the misinformed rantings of individuals who wish for a simpler time and are frightened by technology. The major concern should not be the presence of the microcomputer per se, but the evaluation of software and how it is being put to use. This is particularly true in educational settings. These devices have great potential for being significant learning aides because they are able to present information in a manner that is extremely difficult or impossible to duplicate with traditional methods. In many ways, it is not unlike the use of other audiovisual materials such as film strips, which can be used either to heighten student interest and portray information for discussion or as a pacifier with their cartoon-like or movie-like qualities. Thus, the issue is one of utilization, not simply presence or absence. Again, from my own experience in watching children who have good teachers and well-designed curriculum, the microcomputers enhance communication because these children are able to share pleasurable experiences, such as solving problems using the computer, and pragmatic experiences such as obtaining assistance from other children on the process and pitfalls of utilizing the microcomputer. This is a very fruitful area of research. Many researchers and clinicians interested in the problem of more fully integrating children who are on the fringes of their school and/or social groups into the normal ongoing activities and interchanges, view cooperative use in a systematic fashion of the microcomputer as a potentially useful intervention. However, in the absence of substantial research in this area at the moment, the caution should be that the microcomputer is simply a very sophisticated toy to many children. Unfortunately, the same is true for many intervention agents. However, most children enjoy using it, and if the goals of therapy are well-stated with appropriate assessment and evaluation procedures used (just as would be the case for any intervention), then indeed the microcomputer can be a useful tool.

SPECIALIZED ASSESSMENT

For those working with severely impaired populations, assessment is often a difficult task because standard instruments are of limited value. One often must seek a molecular analysis that involves presenting either an analog or an actual subsection of a learning or performance situation. This is not, however, generally an area for the novice microcomputer user. Most of the applications would entail at one end of the spectrum, the duplication of standard relay-rack equipment for highly-controlled operant learning analyses. A good example of this would be to assess hearing in a child who is extremely difficult to assess. This type of situation has arisen in my laboratory over the years, especially with reference to autistic children. The basic paradigm is a simple one of teaching a discrimination in which the Sd (discriminative stimulus) is key light on and S^ (S delta, indicating non-reinforcement) is key light off. Using a simple response panel connected to the computer, it is an easy task to program the various schedules, to record the response rate, and to summarize the results. One then overlays a tone with the Sd so that a pairing is formed. Then gradually, over many sessions, the intensity of the light is reduced until it is completely absent. At this point, one has the tone coming on and off at random durations and random intertrial intervals just as had been the case with the light. Now, if responding is maintained, one can say that the child does indeed hear. At this point, the long and difficult task of utilizing tones of different frequencies and decibel levels is required to obtain an accurate picture of the child's hearing ability.

Similar paradigms can be used for other forms of assessment. While such assessment can certainly be performed either manually or with standard relay-type equipment, it is much easier to utilize the microcomputer if, as is always the caveat, this is an ongoing activity, not an infrequent event. Setting up the hardware for the first time is the most difficult, as is producing the first software program. However, after that point, it is easy to modify the program so that it records each session's information for each child and allows specific parameters to be changed individually. The system is flexible, easy to use (especially for paraprofessionals), and is highly accurate in the conduct of the procedures. This can result in time saved, and it meets the general cost–benefit requirement of the microcomputer system.

FIGURE 12.1. A typical computer-assisted instruction station. The computer verbally presents a word that the child then is to spell using the keyboard. A correct answer causes the cartoon character to dance to a musical accompaniment. (This software and speech synthesis hardware is produced by Street Electronics—see reference section).

A second example of specialized assessment is the separation of the child's history of learning through interaction with adults from the specific ability to perform learning tasks. Anthony Plienis, former graduate student, and I have been engaged in this research for a number of years and have established a paradigm by which a microcomputer system has been designed to present various learning tasks in a manner analogous to that done by a teacher. The computer has full speech synthesis and thus can provide instructions and feedback, and can present the task within a variety of different teaching strategies. By having the child participate in this type of learning environment while receiving typical teacher instruction, we are able to begin to separate the qualities of the task that have been confounded with the presence of the instructor in the past. The results are beginning to indicate that there are subgroups of children who are responding to aspects of their social learning history. What had been conceptualized as important parameters of the learning task, such as pacing, difficulty level, reinforcement parameters, fading versus trial and error, and so forth, may not be the central parameters in some cases. As the microcomputer system allows us to individualize tasks for each child and to record appropriate session information, this low-cost procedure can be replicated across many children and, combined with classroom observations, will allow us to make what appear (at present) to be strong predictive statements. Thus, for certain child populations, an automated screening system that will help accurately predict the optimal learning environment is not infeasible. However at present, such applications are clearly more appropriate for a research program than for an applied program because we simply do not yet have sufficient information to make general recommendations.

DIRECT INSTRUCTION

As is clear from the previous two sections, the potential use of the microcomputer system for direct instruction with children is very good. The characteristics of a good instructional system include appropriate assessment, individualization of difficulty level and teaching methodology, and continuous assessment of progress with appropriate feedback to alter teaching parameters. These are all components that lend themselves well to computerization. However, as is the case with using the computer to form clinical conclusions or assist in the diagnostic process, these uses are predicated on the presence of sound, well-tested algorithms. It is only once we establish the clear effectiveness of certain teaching approaches can we take the important parameters, translate them to computer software, and then utilize this software for habilitative and therapeutic purposes. All too often, especially within the educational software market, what passes for effective teaching software is simply a lot of visual and auditory stimulation. The majority of these programs do not permit individualization, have minimal if any record-keeping ability that would provide important information about child performance, are repetitive, and have no provision for allowing the instructor to alter important parameters. The promise here is great for effective and appropriate utilization of this technology, but at present, the user must be extremely cautious and skeptical concerning direct instruction application.

Chapter 13
The Physically Handicapped Client

OVERVIEW

Fortunately, after a long history of relative unresponsiveness, clinicians are beginning to provide services for the subsection of physically handicapped populations who are in need of counselling and therapeutic programs. Beyond the obvious boundaries of bias and lack of emphasis and experience in graduate training programs, clinicians have often had difficulty in communicating effectively with the physically handicapped, either because the individual's handicap caused inability to verbally communicate or inability to have sufficient control over their environment in order to exercise some degree of independence due to lack of mobility and dexterity. Examples of this would include quadriplegics and individuals with cerebral palsy. The needs of the physically handicapped are quite diverse with respect to habilitation, rehabilitation, and psychological services, just as they are for any heterogeneous classification of individuals. However, as mentioned, two major categories of need include communication and control over the environment, which are in fact highly related. Thus, as a general approach, the use of microcomputers tends to be a broad-based one, and the microcomputer should be seen as a generalized tool, rather than one to be used for a very specific purpose.

EQUIPMENT MODIFICATION

Typically the computer hardware must be modified in some way to permit the physically handicapped client to use it with ease. The most obvious modification concerns the keyboard. For many individuals, the standard keyboard requires a level of manual dexterity that is not feasible. For many years, a simple modification has been to connect a switch closure mechanism to one of the input ports on the computer. Thus, the keyboard is not replaced, but simply bypassed. One can mount microswitches that require very little pressure to operate in various positions to allow the individual to operate the switch with perhaps a side movement of the head, movement of the chin forward into the switch, a movement of the arm, foot, calf, and so forth. The requirement is that there is some degree of voluntary muscle control and that it is sufficient to activate such a switch.

BASIC COMMUNICATION

This hardware modification is very easy and inexpensive. However, it has the drawback that it places great constraints on the software that can be utilized. That is, the software must be of a scanning mode type. Its basic feature is that a wide variety of options are indicated in a menu format on the video screen. Perhaps the most commonly seen is a simple display of the letters of the alphabet. The software then moves the cursor at a moderate pace to each letter of the alphabet sequentially, where it pauses briefly. As the cursor pauses at each letter, if the user's switch is depressed, this letter is chosen and displayed at the bottom of the screen and placed sequentially in the left-to-right format. Because the user is assembling individual letters into words, conceptually, this is not at all different than the use of a word processor.

The major difficulty with this scanning type approach is its slow speed. It takes quite some time to assemble words because the user is simply choosing in a binary format. That is, one accepts the letter or does not accept the letter as the cursor moves in its predetermined sequence. If one needed the letter "c" to spell the word "call," one would wait until the cursor moved to the "c," press the button, and would then have to wait as the cursor moved throughout the rest of the alphabet and returned to the letter "a." Needless to say, this can be a very frustrating and cumbersome method of communication. However, to an individual with extremely restricted communicative skills in other modalities, it can also be a very exciting experience.

If one becomes more sophisticated with respect to the software, one could adopt a more complex scanning mode. For instance, the program might display the letters of the alphabet on four separate lines, similar to a typewriter keyboard, and have the cursor initially move vertically to each of the four lines. The microswitch is used to indicate what line the letter is on, and then scanning takes place in the more typical format. Modifications of this basic theme can be utilized to provide the user with more and more control over the scanning process to make it faster and more precise. There is a point of diminishing returns, though, as the scan time required among the different options can become as cumbersome as in the first example.

However, with appropriate training, and if it is possible to allow for several microswitches, each representing different functions, their combinations can serve to dramatically increase the speed of communication. In general, the impediment to efficient use of the microcomputer as a communication system is typically not the hardware, but rather the software and the number of different responses that can be transmitted to the computer.

For the physically handicapped client who is also intellectually impaired, different methods of communication are required. The same general approach however, is appropriate. Instead of letters of the alphabet, one can quite readily present graphic representations of various choices and desired activities. Examples would be to place symbols on the screen for various foods or beverages; symbols for a phonograph, radio or television; a symbol to indicate change, such as to change the channel or change the record; symbols to indicate emotions such as happy, sad, confused, and so on. Here, the computer is serving as a translator which allows simple response input to indicate various complex communicative functions by giving an individual the ability to move and stop the cursor at the desired location.

ENVIRONMENTAL CONTROL

As a further extension of the ideas just presented, the computer is also capable of controlling other devices. It is a relatively easy task to utilize the type of scanning system mentioned above to indicate choices that affect the environment, such as turning on various appliances, dialing the telephone, controlling the temperature in a room, and in general, operating a variety of mechanical and electrical devices. This hardware is readily available and is found in most computer retail stores. Indeed, its most common function is as part of security systems designed to turn on and off various lights in particular sequences at certain times of day. It also serves as a sophisticated energy management system to control when heating systems or cooling systems engage in order to reduce expenses (e.g., turning the hot water heater on only in the evening when electricity rates are low). What is important, however, is that these devices are designed to control other devices in the environment. It is irrelevant from the computer's point of view whether it is operating a motor that turns the fan in the heating system or a motor that allows one to raise and lower the blinds.

Perhaps the ultimate form of microcomputer controlled environmental manipulation is the personal robot. Quite different from the industrial robot that has made an entry into the work place, the personal robot is conceptualized as being capable of more generic functioning and flexible programming. I believe that the next year or two will bring great strides in this area. There are currently about half a dozen types of personal robots available to the consumer. In many ways these devices are primitive, but they display many of the basic features necessary for them to serve as a tool for the physically handicapped individual. Without question, animals such as seeing eye dogs and trained rhesus monkeys have been trained to help the physically handicapped. However, although training programs for these animals are sophisticated and quite successful, there remains gaps in their capabilities and in their consistency of performance. The possibility of a personal robot directly under the control of a handicapped individual is quite exciting and will no doubt have some profound influences on the way handicapped individuals view themselves, their handicap, and their relationship to the environment. The control of such a ''mobile generic tool'' should produce an unparalleled degree of freedom and control that was previously impossible. However, the emotional interface between person and computer/robot may not be entirely without problem and may be analogous to some of the psychological dependency and fear associated with mechanical heart recipients and the devices which control the heart. This area of man/machine interface certainly contains far more speculation and conjecture than well-controlled research. Hopefully this will change, as it may indeed be the case that certain elements of this technology will not be beneficial from the perspective of the emotional development and well being of the individual. In the absence of significant research and appropriate assessment procedures, such activities will have to proceed on a case-by-case basis, and what was once speculative science fiction is now becoming very much a reality.

SPEECH SYNTHESIS

The accurate reproduction of human speech has long been an area of great engineering focus. Most early attempts produced speech that was robot-like and proved quite difficult to understand unless placed in a context. As few as five years ago, high-quality speech synthesis was technically possible, although the costs were quite high. However, at present, this technology has become extremely inexpensive. One sees its manifestation in wrist watches that speak and also in automated checkout counters at supermarkets. The difficulty with much of this high-quality speech synthesis is that it is programmed, not open ended. That is, a few words are chosen for an elaborate and complicated encoding process that breaks the speech into component wave forms, digitizes them, applies certain mathematical functions, and stores the information, typically in a ROM. Thus, the device can speak only these few words. In contrast, there are devices known as text-to-speech processors that permit anything that is typed into the keyboard to be spoken by the speech synthesizer. The quality, though, is robot-like and not generally acceptable. However, over the past year, there have been a number of significant changes. The range of human-quality voice has increased dramatically such that it is now possible to buy a speech synthesizer for under $200 that can pronounce over 700 words in a full human quality format. This then permits an interesting adaptation for the basic scanning communication methodology. The individual who cannot communicate verbally can choose words and phrases from a menu and have them produced by the speech synthesizer rather than spelled out on the screen. A fairly wide variety of phrases, especially commonly-used ones, can be displayed on the screen, and with a few movements of the cursor, the user can give complicated instructions to individuals in the immediate environment. The advantage of this method is that others in the environment need not be looking at the computer screen—they can be engaged in other activities.

Current speech synthesis technology is rather sophisticated and certainly will be further refined and improved in the future. Such devices will probably become almost standard on microcomputers, as costs and physical size are reduced.

VOICE RECOGNITION

Another related development that is not quite as far along technologically, is voice recognition. This is the inverse of speech synthesis and requires the computer to analyze the wave forms of the user's incoming speech, translate them into a known vocabulary set, and then execute the commands. There are commercial devices available at the moment that cost approximately $1000 and permit "hands free" operation of the computer. I have been working with such devices for some time now and find that they do function quite well. One drawback, however, is that one must put these devices through what is essentially a learning process. First, a word is spoken into a microphone, which is connected to the device installed in the computer. The device then analyzes this word and breaks it into its component parts. The word is then repeated several times and a generalization curve is produced. As other words are added in a similar fashion, it is sometimes necessary to juxtapose two words to allow the device to make a discrimination between the two. Thus, the words "water" and "juice" would be readily distinguishable by the device. There would be a small error rate associated with the words "come" and "comb," and of course the device could not discriminate between the words "red" and "read." This process of teaching the device is somewhat tedious and requires some skill both on the user's part and on the programmer's part. Because the device is learning a particular voice pattern, it is necessary that the device be taught the individual user's voice pattern. As these patterns can be stored on a diskette and are easily retrieved, one computer could serve several individuals, although not simultaneously. This technology is still relatively new and great improvement can be expected especially given clear economic pressures outside the area of rehabilitation. That is, the needs and desires within the business community to enable users to enter information into the computer verbally rather than manually will have many positive outgrowths for physically handicapped individuals.

Chapter 14
Outcome Evaluation

ORGANIZATION

Outcome evaluation or program evaluation does not significantly change if one is using a microcomputer to assist in the process. In many respects the computer serves a number of the functions mentioned in previous chapters, such as word processing for the preparation of reports and instructions to staff or clients and a data base to accumulate the information of interest. What is important is the organization and structure that is utilized to accumulate evaluative information. The typical concerns for the validity and reliability of the information collected, its frequency of collection, and the specific methodology for the collection of data are governed by the standards of objective evaluation. It is wise, however, that while in the process of determining the organization and structure for evaluation, one considers the limitations and capabilities of the microcomputer system. All too often, the microcomputer is perceived as a way of establishing program credibility through rigorous evaluation. What is often underestimated is the capabilities of the hardware and software with respect to processing large amounts of information.

For example, if one was attempting to keep track of habilitative program progress in a large facility for the developmentally disabled, or in like manner, progress made in group psychotherapy in a large facility for in-patient psychiatric care, one must be sensitive to the amount and frequency of the data collected. Assume that, as an example, one was collecting information for 200 residents, each of whom had an average of from 10 to 15 habilitative programs, and each program produced from one to several dozen pieces of information daily that had to be organized by activity, staff, and shift. One can see that these figures are multiplicative. This is a great deal of information that would take some time to enter into the computer and usually would require the intermediary process of the initial information being transferred to paper and then using this paper to enter the information into the computer. Often the expectation is that staff will perform this function as part of their normal routines. However, one

108

may have to contend with the movement of staff members to where the computer is located and the degree of the software's user-friendliness must be considered. If, in contrast, responsibility for entering is an administrative task, then all the information must be funneled to a central source and a particular person or small group of persons made responsible. This is often the most cost-efficient from the point of view of user entry and lowered error rate, but it certainly has a high cost with respect to staff dedicated to this single purpose.

A distinction must also be made with respect to viewing evaluation as a statement concerning the overall functioning of habilitative programming versus using evaluation on a frequent and ongoing basis to provide feedback for modification of an individual's habilitative or therapeutic program. In the former case, the microcomputer is used in a straightforward manner with respect to word processing and a data base to simply accumulate existing information, analyze it, and present it in a series of written reports, tables, and graphs. This usage is common as there is no special software or hardware required, and the computer is simply a tool for efficient management.

However, as in the second example for clinical management, the requirements are quite different. One is not typically storing information about treatment outcome (such as what percentage of goals were addressed in occupational therapy in the last six months) or staffing patterns on a group basis, but rather one is concerned about the particular pattern of progress or lack thereof for individual habilitative programs for individual clients. In this case whether or not one is referring to such clinical evaluation taking place in a large treatment facility or in a small private practice, many of the variables are the same. One is analyzing patterns that may be temporal, sequential, or cyclical and is also evaluating behavior change that may be specific to a particular intervention, whether it be chemotherapy, group therapy, systematic desensitization, or any other form of intervention. Here very specific software programs are required that often must be custom designed or must utilize sophisticated data-base programs.

A CASE EXAMPLE

By using a series of microcomputers and sophisticated customized software, we have been able to combine clinical evaluation and program evaluation at the Children's Unit for Treatment and Evaluation at SUNY-Binghamton. As an overview, the main steps in the service delivery system include the creation of the Individual Education Plan (IEP), the translation of each of the individual goals into a written habilitative program format that describes in detail the staff requirements, teaching methodologies, materials needed, and the specific parameters of the teaching and social interchange between the instructor and child. Next, each of these individual habilitative programs is placed into a data base that records information on the goal's priority, the time frame for its implementation, the staff member responsible, the specific area of development being addressed, pre-intervention assessment information, group size, teaching methodology, and posttest performance and group size. This data base is then used to produce reports on the current status of each child.

The essential element to this system is that the computer assists in the collation and formatting of the initial IEP. Staff members interact with a user-friendly system that permits them to choose goals and teaching methodologies, materials, priorities, and so forth from a menu-style format. The system has saved innumerable hours in this important process and has resulted in highly organized and easy-to-understand documents. The computer is able to transfer this information to other software programs, each having specific functions, such as preparation of individual habilitative program monitoring forms and reports. Thus, there is little redundancy from the user's point of view, but there are a multitude of applications. In particular, reports can be generated for diverse purposes. One report is prepared for parents to describe the flow of goals that will be addressed over the course of the year. A second more detailed report provides the staff with information concerning sequencing and priority of goals as well as the methodologies to be used for intervention. A separate administrative report organizes each child's information according to the area of development being addressed. Then within each area, it stipulates when programs commence, how many days they have been in effect, staff members responsible for implementation, the response modality, and the criteria that have been set for considering each program successful. This format is similar to an "aged accounting" format. By flagging those programs that have been in effect for greater than 30 days, greater than 60 days, greater than 90 days, and so forth, it assists supervisors in detecting habilitative programs that are ineffective and require a decision concerning either reevaluating the appropriateness of the goal or the intervention strategy. Other report formats are available as well, including a final summary report that provides information for each child concerning degree of success and percentage of goals accomplished which are categorized as successful, partially successful, unsuccessful, and discontinued.

Next in this process, a separate microcomputer system is used to manage all scheduling information for each child. This program allows for easy entry of information concerning physical location within the facility, staff members assigned during each educational period, the names of other children participating in the same group, the number of paraprofessionals available, the specific areas of development being addressed, and the times at which each activity is being conducted for each day of the week. This software program then produces schedule lists that greatly assist staff in the mundane and tedious task of schedule assignment and also produces reports that analyze the amount of time being devoted each week to each area of development, the staff ratio being utilized, and the specific child groupings that are occurring for the purpose of reviewing clinical and educational effectiveness and appropriateness.

Parallel to these various programs, another computer system is used solely for data management purposes. Each habilitative program has a corresponding file in the data management system. For each child, data are entered on daily performance for each program. The system permits rapid and easy data entry and produces three basic types of reports. The first is a graph of the data indicating various condition changes, such as baseline and specific interventions, as well as for absences and periods during which the program was suspended or not conducted. A second report utilizes the same information but presents it in a statistical format. For each of the segments of data that are broken down into logical units, such as baseline, intervention 1, intervention 2, and generalization, the report indicates the number of data points, the minimum, maximum, and mean, as well as the standard deviation. Each of the raw data points are then printed in tabular form containing start date of the program, the IEP goal being addressed, the title of the program, and the criteria that were set in the IEP. Such reports provide a useful counterpart to the graphic analysis and form the basis for detailed review of individual progress. A third type of report is also generated that is more administrative in nature. It scans each child's file and produces a listing of programs that are active and/or those that have been terminated, and for each of them lists their start date, end date, title, the criteria, and the number of data points currently entered. Since there is a data point entered for each school day, just by knowing the current consecutive school day, one can readily determine if the files are up to date.

An on-line, dedicated microcomputer is used to link all rooms and teaching areas within our facility. A series of 12 video display terminals are contained in the various staff offices, classrooms, workrooms, teaching areas, research areas, and administrative offices. Each terminal uses an intercom touch-tone telephone that is in each room to query the computer. For instance, if a staff member wishes to know the current medical status of a child with respect to medication, allergies, illnesses, and so forth, the "0" on the phone keypad is pressed and a list of children appear on the terminal, each with a number next to the name. The correct number is then "dialed", and the information appears on the screen. This is the general format for all interactions with the computer—a series of menus that guide the user to the proper choice, so that all that must be done is to "dial" the number of the required function. Various information may be stored for each child, and thus the computer serves as an "electronic file cabinet."

This on-line system has many other functions. It has a clock/timer so that all terminals display the correct time and serve to coordinate events. The staff enter the times at which they wish to be reminded about certain events, such as when medication is to be dispensed, dismissal times, activity schedules, meetings, and so on. At these requested times, the computer displays the message on the screen and also announces the message over the P.A. system. The computer has full speech-synthesis ability and thus can verbally present any information required. Since the daily schedule format for activities is in half-hour modules, the computer announces these half-hour periods to remind staff of general activity changes. It also assists staff in data recording by specifying the correct recording intervals associated with the behavior-monitoring system employed. The computer times 5-minute segments that serve as the intervals for data recording. It verbally announces these intervals by number each hour (i.e., intervals 1–12) and alerts the staff at the beginning of each hour to begin a new data set. Such a system frees the staff from attending to stop watches or other timing devices and eases the task of data recording. Further, menus are programmed to indicate each child and a wide range of possible target behaviors. When an incident such as a seizure occurs, the staff member dials the child's number and then dials the target behavior. The computer "knows" the time and location of the terminal being used to input this information and thus prints the hardcopy of the incident with this information that can be used for purposes of documentation and staff briefing at shift change. Also, for these special categories of behaviors and incidents (as they are presumed to be serious events), the computer directs this information to all terminals in the facility to alert support and supervisory personnel that an incident is occurring. Recently, this computer has been given "eyes" in the form of several video cameras that can be turned on from any terminal location and will overlay the video image onto the current screen display. As an example, a teacher can monitor the arrival and departure of buses from the parking lot and the behavior of the children at that location. The system also coordinates the phone system to relay messages to the staff via the terminals and serves as an electronic bulletin board, displaying various general staff messages, eliminating the need for frequent memos and briefings. Therefore, this on-line system serves a very important component of our communication needs and helps to systemize not only service delivery, but also the evaluation of the delivery process. It permits an easy method for examining patterns of incidents, staff communication, information utilization, and scheduling methods.

This is a complex system that has taken several years to develop, but I believe it states quite well that through proper use of appropriate hardware and software, one can construct a system that meets both specific clinical needs as well as administrative and program evaluation requirements. These various needs are met simultaneously and in a harmonious fashion with neither detracting from the other. The impact of such a system can be profound and is illustrated in Figure 14.1.

As can be seen from Figure 14.1, the effect on the number of habilitative programs conducted per child was not initially substantial due to the time necessary to implement the system, to perform the inevitable debugging, and to train staff in its usage. However, as the system became fully implemented, the effect was quite profound. There is a tired phrase among computer users that the goal is to "work better, not harder." This is in fact what occurred in this example. Staff did not spend more hours to achieve this increase in effectiveness, but rather utilized the same amount of time to perform tasks more efficiently and had access to more useful information that, in turn, guided their activities. Thus, while there may be a brief period of increased workload in order to implement what might be termed *a program management computer system*, if it is properly conceptualized and implemented, the effects can be profound and very cost-efficient.

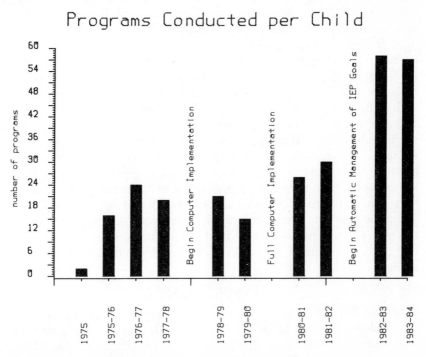

FIGURE 14.1. The effect of various phases of computer implementation on the number of habilitative programs conducted in a facility for developmentally disabled children.

Chapter 15
The Double-Edged Sword

As with any new technology or methodology, there is always a period of conflict and debate as the technology is tested, assessed, and, if found to be valuable, integrated into the mainstream. The utilization of computer technology certainly has a cost–benefit conflict associated with it, particularly within the realm of human services. For the non-applied research psychologist, computer technology has been extremely helpful in the direct conduct of research, especially in the areas of enhancing laboratory control and facilitating data analysis. It is quite common to find microcomputers in psychological laboratories that focus on human factors, memory and cognition, perception, neuropsychology, and psychobiology. In these areas, the computer is an important tool and functions in a manner analogous to earlier breeds of laboratory equipment, such as the venerable relay rack which taught many of us the pragmatic side of logical analysis. However, clinical endeavors in psychology for the most part do not have a history of technology utilization. One caricature of clinical psychology is that the clinician simply requires a few comfortable chairs, an office, and a note pad in order to effectively deliver services. There have been recent influences with respect to biofeedback and behavioral assessment, because there are elements of current technology being proposed and utilized very effectively. Nevertheless, I believe it is important from an historical perspective to note that clinical activities have more often than not been considered the ''art form'' of psychology and have not been easily quantified and analyzed. Certainly there are many schools of thought on this matter and while there is indeed a continuum, as an overall evaluation of clinical practice (and even of clinical research), it is not noted for its rigor.

ASSESSMENT

Against this backdrop of historical perspective it is also important to note that traditionally, clinical psychologists have been viewed as individuals who administer tests and, only more recently, as the direct providers of therapeutic services. Most contemporary clinical psychologists reject this characterization and they tend to downplay the importance of assessment.

In fact, many practicing clinicians consider this an area of drudgery compared to the more exciting issues surrounding intervention. From my own perspective, assessment is a critical, inseparable, and ongoing component of intervention. It is also true, however, that assessment procedures, whether standardized instruments, projective tests, or behavioral assessment procedures, require constant honing of skills and great diligence to administer.

Part and parcel of assessment is the continuing evaluation by the psychologist of both the specific and nonspecific responses to the assessment procedures and a continuing application of clinical judgement and experience to interpret what is occurring. When computer technology is used beyond a simple scoring of the instrument to produce numeric and graphic analysis, a very dangerous situation can occur. It is interesting to note that virtually without exception, the computer programs available from a variety of sources, despite great claims made for their accuracy and effectiveness, are designed to score only a single assessment instrument. That is, for a given instrument such as the WISC-R, elaborate analyses and conclusions are often presented about the significance of the scores and their pattern. But what clinician would base conclusions on a single instrument? Clearly one attempts to synthesize information from many different sources both historical and current, and this is simply not achieved with current computer "interactive" scoring. I have been very distressed by the presence of such computer-generated reports in the files of both children and adults. While "efficiency" can be vastly increased (i.e., a given school district might be able to significantly reduce its backlog of testing for handicapped children, or a clinician in a psychiatric facility for adults might be able to prepare the required annual psychological report much faster), the responsibility to make appropriate judgements and to synthesize information still rests with the clinician. Often the marketing for computer assessment and treatment programs implies that they mimic the clinical process and in some ways can improve upon that process. This is indeed false, as the current status of such programs are that they do not mimic the clinical process, but rather serve to extensively analyze only one or a very few components of the process. In my opinion, these programs often overgeneralize from this limited information. I find little comfort in the disclaimer that accompanies such software that warns the user that the information produced should be used only as a guide. Were this indeed the desired outcome, vendors would not format the printed reports to emulate the appearance of standard written reports.

DOCUMENTATION

Also of concern is the practice of using the computer to generate a "smoke screen", or the illusion of credibility. In the last decade, there has been growing emphasis upon credibility and empirical evaluation of both service delivery and service outcome. Because of its high speed and flexibility, a computerized system can easily be perverted to provide voluminous "documentation" that bears little or no resemblance to the actual processes taking place. That is, one can produce very detailed treatment plans and detailed schedules of activities, history of interventions, and lengthy monthly reports that are but facades. Because of its capabilities to produce documents in an impressive-looking format, an illusion of efficiency and validity can be generated.

Unfortunately, for many individuals there remains a sense of awe and a distinct bias that computer-generated information connotes validity. This conclusion is often based on the partial knowledge that the computer utilizes logic, that logic is objective, and therefore the information being received is objective. Certainly in my work, when various regulatory and review bodies evaluate services not as a function of improvement in the condition of the individual, but rather with documentation that certain events and procedures have transpired, that quality control has little meaning. It has always been a very sobering thought as I prepare documents for such bodies to know that with little difficulty, one could easily produce the extensive documentation requested by utilizing the computer and at the same time provide totally inadequate clinical services. It is because of such concerns that I strongly advocate rigorous clinical outcome and program evaluation procedures. There must be objective, verifiable information concerning service delivery that is separate from the simple paper documentation that occurs along with the process of service delivery.

THE PROCESS OF
DISCRIMINATION

As is true in most cases, the answers to the questions raised are not simply yes or no, but rather they involve issues of determining for which situations and activities the use of computer technology is appropriate. Recently I have become aware of a psychologist who is practicing "psychotherapy at a distance" utilizing the computer. That is, the clients use their computers to tie into the therapist's computer via a modem. The "session" takes place via this keyboard interchange. Clients can also dial the therapist's computer and request that a variety of informational booklets about certain clinical topics be sent to them. Billing is accomplished through assessing a fee for each word received and transmitted by the therapist.

My initial reaction to this type of arrangement is, very strongly, negative. I have heard arguments that perhaps there are individuals who would feel more comfortable conversing with a therapist in this electronic fashion and thus, would be receiving assistance where normally they would not. Additional arguments suggest that this approach is received negatively simply because it is novel and that using such technology in no way compromises the therapeutic process, but simply reflects the reality of our times. These arguments, however, do not seem compelling. My clinical orientation strongly rejects the notion of clinical services as an art form. I believe that they are an extension of the basic research findings in the field of psychology and related areas. Nevertheless, I consider face-to-face contact with the client to be crucial. This brings us back to the issue previously raised: What information is the clinician drawing upon in order to formulate hypotheses and to proceed with clinical services? This information is not unidimensional. It involves a multitude of factors that are not often easily articulated. Nevertheless they are present, and to restrict the interchange to a highly-filtered or limited modality such as telecommunications, wherein the only method of analysis is the content and syntax of the message being both received and provided by the therapist, I believe, is not a defendable position.

There is a parallel here to some of the issues raised in chapter 12 with respect to direct instruction with children. Computer programs that help instruct children in various academic tasks or that promote acquisition of certain concepts may seem very valid to the casual observer, but all too often there is little substance to these programs. Appropriate research has not yet revealed the best teaching methodologies for children with specific disorders and disabilities. In the absence of conclusive research findings, how is it possible to design computer teaching programs? I believe the answer is clear (and it applies to many other areas in which computer technology is being used to "assist" in the clinical process): The computer is simply an extension of a particular individual or small group of individuals who "believe" they have found an answer. This type of egocentric approach based upon "clinical experience" rather than well-executed research is not new to our profession. However, the medium has indeed changed. Previously, such approaches were disseminated through books and in particular, were marked several years ago by the explosive growth of the "self-help" paperbacks. Many decried this type of dissemination to a public unsophisticated and uncritical with regard to issues concerning validity. This period also saw the growth of "pop" psychology and its unfortunate influence.

Perhaps the current wave of computer software geared for "automated" assessment and therapy, and the various self-help software appearing now that "guarantees" successful treatment of obesity, insight into one's "inner mind" or in-depth analysis of other individuals (such as one's business rival) are similar to the self-help books and the writings of the popular press. Perhaps this old problem has simply taken on the trappings of a newer medium. Perhaps it is a passing fad that will soon fade.

I think not. I base my pessimism on the impression that the computer provides a very different medium from that of a book or pamphlet. Printed material provides essentially a passive medium. The individual can read the material, but cannot query it. A skilled author may anticipate such questions and organize the material accordingly, but the book will nevertheless remain a passive medium. In contrast, the computer presents an interactive medium. A grand illusion is created that the computer appears to be responding to the queries of the individual and appears to be making decisions, thus, providing answers. One of perhaps the oldest attempts at artificial intelligence with computers is a program known as Eliza. This program was developed many years ago and has evolved into many different forms. Interestingly, this program supposedly serves as an attempt to mimic the process that takes place in nondirective psychotherapy. The program is indeed fascinating to utilize and in some circumstances it portrays very well the illusion that one is conversing with a therapist. Its function at one level is not difficult to comprehend or to duplicate. The computer accepts text input from the keyboard and matches this input to a stored list of vocabulary. As it scans for certain words such as "depressed," "angry," "lonely," and so forth, it matches these with predetermined phrases, such as "Why do you feel that you are . . . ?," to "reflect" back to the user. Because of this ability to mimic communication, if the software documentation does not explicitly provide detailed explanation of its operation, its effects can be at best a curiosity or a form of entertainment, and at worst a source of great potential harm.

SAFEGUARDS

There should be several levels of protection for the public. One should be the judgement and ethics of the professional not to use clinically-oriented computer software inappropriately. I believe that the majority will act responsibly and will treat the emergence of such software no differently than the introduction of new assessment materials. Evaluations will be based on standardization data concerning reliability and validity of the various instruments. This will not be sufficient, however, as there are already indications of misuse and there is little consolation that perhaps most of the misuse is occurring because of naïveté.

Thus, a second level of protection should occur through the development of appropriate standards for such software. This process has begun both within APA and among private vendors who share these concerns. The establishment of formal written standards similar to those that currently exist from APA for assessment instruments will do much to stabilize the field and provide appropriate reference points. Nonetheless, in my opinion, this still will not be sufficient. Therefore, a third level of protection is required. As discussed previously, the difficulty is not in software that simply provides a quick method of scoring tests, but rather in software that interprets clinical information. Such software has the potential to be of great use to the clinician as well as to the applied researcher, but only if the specific algorithms used in the software are made available to the user. The logic and specific rules utilized to present judgements based upon the information that is input by the user should be available to the user. Most software vendors have rejected such suggestions, stating that it is not possible. They are concerned about proprietary information and fear that by divulging their particular method others will copy it. This is perhaps the essence of the difficulty. The norm for clinical decision making is to share with colleagues the exact basis for decisions. For this reason, we have conventions, seminars, workshops, and we engage in supervised clinical training. Thus, computer applications within the clinical area have a potential for great harm because currently they engage in only half the process. In other words, the software disseminates conclusions but not the process, the choice points, and the basis for the conclusions. Business and monetary concerns are simply insufficient to outweigh what I believe is a critical issue in professional and ethical conduct in clinical service delivery.

The concern about proprietary information is somewhat predictable given that most individuals producing such clinically oriented software are new to the software industry. For many years these issues have been discussed among traditional software vendors and they are beginning to learn that elaborate protection schemes inflate the cost of software and do not protect the vendor. As the general industry of software production comes of age, one hopes that some of the harsh lessons learned will be incorporated by specialized vendors. However, the majority of these vendors tend to be relatively small and, thus, perhaps have a disproportionate fear of infringement and piracy. The real issue underlying these difficulties may be that the concern falls within the arena of business rather than the arena of ethics and professional conduct. As an example, I am involved in a long-term project of creating an "expert" system specifically designed to assist clinicians in the treatment of self-injurious behavior. This project has grown out of my own frustration from many years of seeing the limitations on the abilities of training seminars, workshops, in-service programs, and so on, to transmit the necessary skills to individuals in the service delivery system to adequately treat severe cases of self-injury. The difficulty is that this behavior pattern is complex and unresponsive to typical intervention in its severe forms. The information that must be collected for assessment as well as the specifics and timing of intervention are complex enough that the process is not amenable to the relatively brief training interchanges that take place in workshops or even extended in-service training. However, there is indeed a logic, methodology, and a set of information that is important and useful for effective treatment. Given the current status of both hardware and software development, it is possible for a skilled clinician to begin to transfer this logic and information to an appropriately interactive software program. It is a fascinating process and helps to clarify and crystallize the approach of the clinician by forcing the explicit articulation of the process and putting it into a logical format that the computer can then execute. Once this is done, it should be a very useful and efficient software program. That is my expectation at this point, and I am optimistic for its validity. However, this is an empirical question and must be tested. This software will explicitly give the decision rules for all the various choice points and, in this regard, will be no different than the process that occurs in face-to-face consultation or in teaching workshops. The difference will be in the medium and in the fact that the interchange with the computer will be less open-ended than in face-to-face consultation.

From this perspective it may be clear why I feel so strongly about the necessity for disclosure of the algorithms and decision rules, and why I do not believe software producers should be concerned about losses as a result of these disclosures. The reason for this is that this information is proprietary in exactly the same way as it would be if it was a published document or presented at a public meeting. Guidelines for plagiarism exist and the ability of our profession to deal with instances of plagiarism will serve us as well for computer software as it has for printed and verbal dissemination. It is because of the misplaced perception that there is something magical or different about the computer, rather than viewing it as simply another medium or tool, that is creating these feelings of concern and distrust among many software vendors. Even a high risk of "piracy" of the ideas and concepts contained in such clinically oriented software packages would be insufficient justification for not providing the basic decision-making algorithms and information. Once again, this is a clinical endeavor and individual clinicians must have access to this information to fully understand the implications of the output being provided by the software and thus, in turn, they will be able to weigh the computer output with respect to the decisions made concerning services for a given individual.

ENTHUSIASM

After detailing many of the concerns and pitfalls of applying computer technology to the clinical process, it is important to place these concerns within an overall positive context. Certainly I have great enthusiasm for this technology and as with any technology or methodology, there will be instances of abuse against a background of great benefit. Indeed my enthusiasm is unbridled for this technology, as I believe it will very significantly alter the work habits and efficiency of psychologists and others in allied fields who are engaged in clinical practice, research, teaching, and administration. The microcomputer is such a powerful generic tool that it can quickly become assimilated into the day-to-day fabric of one's activities. For this to happen however, the novice must engage in a careful self-assessment, spend time investigating specific hardware and software, and adopt a systematic program of learning the necessary skills. Certainly one should not be discouraged by the initial learning curves, nor by the jargon and the apparently constant changing technology. As the user's skills improve and as an impact is made on the workload, more and more time becomes available for the activities that are most productive and enjoyable, and which allow this tool to be used for purposes of innovation and development of new problem-solving skills.

Glossary

Italicized terms are defined in the glossary.

Acoustic coupler   A *modem* with two rubber cups to hold the handset of the telephone firmly.

A-D   Analog to digital. Circuitry that converts an analog signal, such as skin conductance, to a digital signal that can be processed by the computer.

Address   The location in *RAM* or *ROM* where a specific set of information is stored. Usually specified by giving a hexadecimal start point in absolute terms followed by the length of the information (e.g., *"Basic* has a starting address at 2D00 with a length of 12.5K.").

Algorithm   The specific steps required to solve a problem. Similar to a *flowchart.* More generally, the conceptualization of the approach used to write *software* for a specific task.

Alpha   The letters of the alphabet as distinguished from numerals.

Alphanumeric   The mixture of numerals, letters, and symbols as found on most keyboards.

Assembly language   A programming language one step above *machine language.* Somewhat cumbersome and difficult to use, but results in programs that execute at high speed.

ASCII   Acronym for American Standard Code for Information Exchange. A system for assigning a specific number (*binary* and decimal as they are complimentary systems) for each digit from 0 to 9, each letter of the alphabet, and assorted symbols. It permits translation of the computer's binary information to our standard system of letters and numbers.

Back-up   A copy of a working program or set of data to guard against loss due to damage to the original.

Basic   Beginners All-Purpose Symbolic Instructional Code, created at Dartmouth in 1964. The first *user-friendly* programming *language.* The most popular programming language for microcomputers. Currently being revamped by its authors.

Baud   A unit of measurement for data communications. Typically used in referring to communication via *modem* or to transferring data to a printer. Dividing by 10 approximates the number of characters per second transmitted. Common values are 300 baud for *modems*, 1,200 for printers, and 9,600 for *CRTs*.

Binary   A number system for which the basic elements are 0 and 1, or "off" and "on." A decimal translation would be as follows:

$$0 = 0 \quad\quad 5 = 101$$
$$1 = 1 \quad\quad 6 = 011$$
$$2 = 01 \quad\quad 7 = 111$$
$$3 = 11 \quad\quad 8 = 0001$$
$$4 = 001 \quad\quad \text{etc.}$$

Bit   A contraction of "binary digit;" its value is either 1 or 0.

Board   a.k.a. card. Short for printed circuit board. A rigid plastic sheet that has wiring etched on its surface and holes to accept the electronic components.

Boot   Originates from "Pulling yourself up by your bootstraps." Typically a short program in *ROM*, that is run when the computer is turned on. It accesses a more complex program on disk, which is loaded and executed, providing the basic operating system.

Branch   Stands for "branching" program; the process of making a decision based upon the values obtained at a choice point. In a software program, if a yes/no answer is required, the program would "branch" to two different sections conditional upon the yes or no response.

Buffer   Typically, a reserved memory space used for the temporary transfer of data between the computer and *peripherals*.

Bug   A small error in a software program or in hardware that results in inconvenience disproportionate to the severity of the error or problem.

Bus   A standard configuration of access points to the *CPU* which permits the addition of certain hardware components, such as memory boards. The bus can both transmit and receive information.

Byte   A basic unit for computer processing indicating the number of *bits* processed simultaneously. Usually refers to 8 bits. Used to refer to memory or storage availability.

Central Processing Unit (CPU)   The true brain of the computer that executes software *instructions*. Serves to control or modulate all other related circuitry in the computer. Often specified by code number (e.g., 6502, 8088, Z80, etc.) Also referred to by number of bits it processes simultaneously (e.g., 8 bit, 16 bit, or 32 bit).

Character   The basic units of interaction with the computer usually via the keyboard. A character is a letter, symbol, single digit, or blank space (e.g., the phrase, "at 1:00 PM" contains 10 characters).

Chip An *integrated circuit*. Name derived from a small silicon wafer onto which the numerous components are etched. The "chip" itself is much smaller than the enclosing case with its "pins" that connect to the circuit board.

Compiler A software program that translates software written in "high-level" languages, such as BASIC or FORTRAN, into machine language programs. The result is that the program will run many times faster.

Computer A device that stores and processes information.

Core An antiquated term referring to the computer's random access memory (RAM).

CP/M Control Program for Microprocessors. A popular operating system for Z80-type microprocessors, often characterized as a business-oriented *operating system*.

Crash The sudden transfer of control of the computer to "never-never land." The system becomes "hung up" and nonresponsive. Analogous to a psychotic break or a coma, depending upon etiology of the crash.

CRT Cathode ray tube. The video monitor or screen of the computer. Does not have a keyboard as an integral component.

Cursor The moving "blob" on the CRT that indicates current position. Has a variety of shapes, the most popular of which is a small, vertically-oriented rectangle.

D-A Digital to analog. See *A-D*.

Daisy Wheel Printer A printer that uses a plastic disk (wheel) that has letters and numbers molded on its surface. Analogous to the type ball on a typewriter. Produces high-quality print identical to a good typewriter.

Data base A collection of data organized into specific *records* and *files*. The records may be accessed in a random sequence for a variety of purposes.

Direct access a.k.a. random access. A process whereby specific information is retrieved directly, rather than as part of a sequential search.

Disk drive A device analogous to a record player except that it can "write" as well as "read" information that is magnetically encoded on a diskette. Allows random access of data as the read/write head can be moved across the diskette in a nonsequential manner just as a phonograph needle can be placed on a specific groove of a record. A hard disk stores much more information and uses a rigid usually nonremovable disk.

Diskette a.k.a. floppy diskette. A thin, circular disk coated with magnetic material. Usually enclosed in a semi-rigid or rigid "envelope." Typical sizes are 5¼" and 8". Used to store large amounts of data.

Error Message A display by the computer when an error is detected. In sophisticated systems, the source and type of error is displayed.

Execute   See *Run*.

Field   A partition of a *record* that is reserved for a specific category and type of information. In a client demographics record, one field would be reserved for last name, one for first name, one for address, and so on.

File   A collection of *records*, each of related information stored as a unit (e.g., a file for client demographics, a file for references related to biofeedback, etc.). Also refers to any information, such as a software program, stored as unit on a diskette.

Firmware   The programs stored in *ROM* which are non-volatile and not user-changeable. Often contains the *boot* program and operating system.

Flowchart   A schematic representation of the steps (*algorithm*) used in a program. More generally, any schematic representation of a process.

FORTRAN   A contraction of Formula Translation. A high-level *language* popular for many years with researchers, used more often on minicomputers than micro-computers.

GIGO   A *hacker* phrase that stands for "garbage in—garbage out." A reference to the notion that the source of errors is the user and not the computer.

Glitch   A hardware malfunction, not necessarily objectively verifiable, that is invoked to explain a computer error or problem that is believed not to be of software origin.

Graphics   A general term that usually refers to an image assembled at the *pixel* level rather than with the standard characters available at the keyboard.

Hacker   A skilled computer programmer/user who displays no anxiety about the person-computer interchange. Not equivalent to the derogatory term "nerd."

Handshaking   The mutual trading of information between two devices to regulate the flow of information. The signals usually include "ready to send," "ready to receive," and "busy."

Hardware   A generic term that refers to the actual components of a computer system such as the *CRT*, *motherboard*, printer, and so on.

Hex   Short for hexadecimal, a base 16 number system whose elements are 0 1 2 3 4 5 6 7 8 9 A B C D E F.

Hollerith card   a.k.a. punch card. An elongated index card that codes information as a series of punched holes in vertical columns. Currently the norm is 80 columns per card. This card system was invented by Herman Hollerith who used it to speed the 1890 census. He founded the Tabulating Machine Corporation, which eventually was incorporated into the International Business Machines Corporation. The Hollerith card was an extension of the punched-card system used by Jacquard to control the patterns produced by automated looms of the early 1800s.

Input   Either a noun that describes information being fed to the computer via keyboard, storage device, or other *peripheral* or a verb that describes the process of entering information into the computer.

Interface   Usually an electronic device that serves as "middleman," permitting compatible operation between two unrelated components, such as the computer and a printer.

Instruction   A command in a programming *language* that has a specific *syntax* and specifies an operation to be performed by the computer.

Integrated circuit   a.k.a. the chip. An electronic device composed of a small, silicon wafer upon which components are etched in a complex process to simulate transistors, capacitors and resistors.

Joystick   Analagous to the joystick in some airplanes. It detects $x - y = $axis movement through a stick or knob the user moves. This motion is used to control certain computer functions such as moving images on the *CRT*.

Key   Variously, to enter information from the keyboard ("key data entry"), a single switch on the keyboard, or the selected *field* in a data *record* that is used to sort and file the data record.

Kilobyte   One thousand bytes of storage space, *RAM* or information. Precisely, it is 1024 bytes. The values are often "rounded"—64K of memory is exactly 65,536 bytes. The approximate values are used when referring to general characteristics of the microcomputer. It is necessary to use the precise figures when calculating the specific storage needs for particular data bases or when performing manipulations upon sub-sections of data arrays.

Language   A comprehensive series of computer *instructions* that have a specific *syntax* that may be combined to produce a complex series of integrated commands. This series is referred to as a program. Examples of languages are BASIC, FORTRAN, LOGO, and PASCAL.

Light pen   A light-sensitive stylus that provides input to the computer, enabling identification of the pen's x–y location on the video screen. Inexpensive pens sense a specific light pattern generated by the computer, are generally slow, and have poor resolution. More sophisticated pens sense the faster scan (the "sweep" of the electron gun across the CRT) and have excellent resolution.

Machine Language   The specific binary language, unique to each type of *CPU*, that can be processed by the CPU directly, without translation. Higher-level languages, such as BASIC or PASCAL, are actually translated to machine language prior to execution. Thus, programs written in machine language execute at high speed, many times faster than high-level languages.

Megabyte   One million bytes, or more precisely, 1,048,576 bytes.

Menu   A list of possible options the user may choose from in a software program. Menu-driven programs are considered more user-friendly than programs requiring the user to use specific commands.

Microcomputer   A small computer that utilizes a microprocessor. It is usually self-contained and complete except for a video display and printer. Once noted for its limited abilities, speed, and memory, such characterizations are no longer applicable.

Microprocessor A generic term for a wide range of integrated circuits (also known as a *CPU*) that contain the basic logic and arithmetic processing circuits along with a *bus* structure to communicate with other integrated circuits. A microprocessor is often classified according to its speed of operation, number of different instructions it can execute, and size of the data bus. Physically, it measures about $\frac{1}{4}" \times 1" \times 2"$, although there is variation within a narrow range.

Minicomputers A predecessor of the microcomputer previously differentiated by its higher speed and memory capacity. The distinction between minicomputers and microcomputers is now blurring and differentiation is now more a matter of specific configuration than inherent qualities.

Modem An acronym for modulator-demodulator. A device that converts digital signals from the computer to tones which can be transmitted over telephone lines. It also converts such tone signals received back to a digital format. Necessary for "tying in" to other remote computers.

Motherboard The main logic circuit board for the microcomputer. The "guts" of the microcomputer. Typically contains the *CPU*, *ROMs*, some *RAM*, character generator, video generation circuitry, and disk controller.

Mouse 1) A small rodent used extensively in psychological research. 2) A small device about the size of a pack of cigarettes that is moved across a desk surface. The mouse senses this movement and in turn moves the cursor in direct proportion to the mouse's movement. A user-friendly interface between software and user input.

Nanosecond One billionth of a second. A unit of measurement appropriate for the speed of operation of microprocessors.

Network A system of interconnecting, independent computers in which each operates autonomously but can share information among any member of the network. It is not *time-sharing*.

Numeric Refers to data that consists only of numbers. Alphanumeric refers to a combination of numeric and alphabet characters.

On-line The status of a *peripheral* device when it is connected to the *CPU* (via an appropriate interface) and is able to communicate with the CPU. A device may be physically connected via cables, but either not powered on or not currently able to communicate with the CPU as the CPU is engaged in other activities or the peripheral is not electronically connected (internal switches or relays set to off). Sometimes confused with *real-time*.

Operating system A host software program that manages the essential functions and interaction of the microcomputer system components. It permits "higher-level" programming *languages* to perform specialized application functions by serving as the interface between application software and the microcomputer.

Operation   An elementary unit of action that the *CPU* can perform, such as arithmetic processes and reading and writing information to memory.

Output   The data or information that the *CPU* directs to the printer, *CRT*, or other *peripheral* as a result of the operation of a command or program.

Parallel   A method of data transmission in which data is sent and received simultaneously, typically 8 *bits* at a time, along a multiconductor cable.

Peripheral   A device external to the *CPU* that extends its functions. Typically refers to printers, *disk drives, modems, plotters*, and similar specialized devices.

Personal Computer   a.k.a. microcomputer. A small, relatively inexpensive computer designed for use by one individual at a time.

Pixel   The smallest point or dot that can be displayed on a *CRT*. Characters, numbers, and graphics are composed of groups of pixels.

Plotter   A device that produces finely detailed line drawings on paper or acetate, typically using a variety of pens equipped with various types and colors of ink. The pen moves in the x-y axes on a flat bed. Drum plotters move the paper in the y-axis and the pen moves in the x-axis, much like a cumulative recorder.

Port   The point of actual hardware connection to the *CPU* that permits communication with other devices.

Program   a.k.a. software program, sometimes abbreviated to software. The assemblage of specific commands that produce a series of interrelated operations of the computer and peripherals that results in a functional output for the user.

QWERTY   An infrequently used term to refer to the standard keyboard configuration of most computers. Derives simply from the first six letters of the alphabet on the first row of the keyboard.

RAM   Random access memory. Volatile memory that allows binary information to be read from and written to specific memory addresses randomly (i.e., any desired sequence).

Read   To retrieve information stored in *RAM*, on *diskettes*, or in some other format or media.

Real-time   Interaction with the computer that is immediate as opposed to delayed, such as placing work to be done in a queue to be processed as time allows.

Record   A series of pieces of information organized into fields and functionally related to one another. It is stored or referenced as a single unit, such as a client's demographic information.

Register   Specific memory locations in the *CPU* itself, used for temporary storage of information.

ROM   Read only memory. Similar to *RAM*, but can only be read, not written to, and is not *volatile*.

RS-232   A standard hardware configuration for *serial* communication.

Run   A command that causes a *program* to execute its sequence of *instructions*. The process that results when a program is executed, that is, it runs.

Screen   a.k.a. *CRT*, video display, monitor, and tube.

Scroll   The illusion of vertical or horizontal movement on a *CRT*. The information on the CRT is rewritten at high speed, shifted one line vertically, or some small unit horizontally.

Sequential   Data stored in a linear format, resulting in slow access time. Magnetic tape is an example of sequential storage.

Serial   A method of data transmission in which data segments are sent and received in sequential format.

Software   A generic term referring to computer programs. Typically loaded into the computer via *disk, tape*, or keyboard. Not equivalent to *firmware*.

Solid state   A generic name for transistorized devices and integrated circuits (microchips). Refers to movement of electrons (electricity) in the solid materials of such devices in contrast to flow across electrodes in vacuum tubes.

Sort   To place data into particular groups or to place data into a specific sequence (e.g., to place a *file* of names into alphabetical order).

Speech Synthesis   Production of varying quality levels of speech, from robot-like to full human sounding speech, through a variety of different techniques. Typically requires additional hardware and software.

Spooling   Data is transmitted at high speed to a reserved section of memory, either internal or external to the computer, which is, in turn, transmitted at a slower rate to a peripheral, such as a printer. Often referred to as printer buffering. Also associated with temporary storage to a *disk file* for later printing or retrieval. All methods permit the *CPU* to continue tasks without being delayed by relatively slower devices.

Store   To transfer data to specific memory locations or to *disk* or *tape*.

Subroutine   An integrated cluster of *instructions* that perform a particular function used routinely by the *program*. A subset of the program.

Syntax error   A nasty little message the computer displays when an instruction is given improperly or with the incorrect parameters. The bane of the novice computer user.

System   Short for computer system. Refers to the *CPU* and all related *peripherals*.

System master   a.k.a. system disk. A *program* used to *boot* the *system* when initially turned on. It provides the initial operating system for the computer.

Tape   A general reference to magnetic tape and tape drives. A formerly popular method of storing very large amounts of data. Now often replaced by *hard disks*.

Terminal   A *CRT* with keyboard.

Time sharing   The multiple use, simultaneously, of a computer. The computer "shares" its time with each user by processing segments of instructions from each user in roughly a rotating fashion (i.e., it is not truely simultaneous but is at such a high speed it appears simultaneous). As the number of users increase, the speed of response to each user usually becomes progressively slower and slower.

VDT   Video display terminal; a *CRT* with keyboard.

Update   Any change made to a set of data.

User-friendly   Software designed for ease of use by unskilled operators. Clearly a relative term.

Utility   An auxiliary program to the *operating* system that performs a routine function, such as displaying memory contents, copying a diskette, or displaying statistics about disk storage usage.

Volatile   An unstable condition. Usually used in reference to *RAM*. Data can be maintained in RAM only with the presence of a constant electric current. When the electricity is turned off, the information is lost.

Winchester disk   a.k.a., a *hard disk*.

Write   To place data in a specific memory location or to transfer data to *disk* or *tape*.

Zap   An "inside" technical term used among *hackers* to indicate the intentional destruction of data or a file. Not to be confused with the nonvolitional destructive results of "bug" and "glitch" and the truly ominous "system crash."

Resources and References

Behavior Observation

C.B.T.A.
1819 Gary Dr.
Vestal, NY 13850

Performax, Inc.
P.O. Box 876
White Plains, NY 10604

Biofeedback/Physiological Measurement

The American Biotechnology Corp.
24 Browning Dr.
Ossining, NY 10562
(914) 762-4646

Cyborg
342 Western Ave.
Boston, MA 02135
(800) 343-4494

Farrall Instruments Inc.
P.O. Box 1037
Grand Island, NB 68802
(308) 385-1530

Interactive Structures, Inc.
146 Montgomery Ave.
Bala Cynwyd, PA 19004
(215) 667-1713

Self Regulation Systems
1477 N.E. 95th St.
Redmond, WA 98052
(206) 882-1101

Bulletin Board

PI-Net
Academic Applications
c/o Dr. Robert Klepac
Dept. of Mental Health
Wilford Hall
Air Force Medical Center
Lackland Airforce Base
San Antonio, TX 78236

Data Analysis

Crunch Software
2547-22nd Ave.
San Francisco, CA 94116
(415) 564-7337

Graphwriter
Graphic Communications, Inc.
200 Fifth Ave.
Waltham, MA 02254
(617) 890-8778

Human Systems Dynamics
9010 Reseda Blvd.
Suite 222
Northridge, CA 91324

Master Chart
Spectral Graphics
540 N. California
Suite 22B
Stockton, CA 95202

Microsoft Chart
Microsoft Corp.
10700 Northup Way
Box 97200
Belkvue, WA 98004
(206) 828-8080

The Prime Plotter
Primesoft Corp.
P.O. Box 30
Calvin John, MD 20818
(301) 229-4229

Data-Base Services

BRS
1200 Route 7
Latham, NY 12110
(800) 833-4707

Dialog Information Services, Inc.
3460 Hillview Ave.
Pala Alto, CA 94304
(800) 227-1927

The Source
Source Telecomputing Corp.
1616 Anderson Rd.
McLean, VA 22102
(800) 336-3366

Data-Base Search Software

In Search
Menlo Corp.
4633 Old Ironsides
Suite 400
Santa Clara, CA 95050
(408) 986-0200

Sci-Mate Searchers
Institute for Scientific Information
3501 Market St.
Philadelphia, PA 19104
(800) 523-4092

Journals/Newsletters/Columns

Computers in Human Behavior
Pergamon Press, Inc.
Maxwell House
Fairview Park
Elmsford, NY 10523
(914) 592-7700

Computers in Human Services
The Haworth Press
28 East 22 St.
New York, NY 10010

Computers in Psychiatry/Psychology
Box 0
26 Trumbull St.
New Haven, CT 06511

MicroPsych Network
Professional Resource Exchange, Inc.
P.O. Box 15560
Sarasota, FL 34277

Newsletter for the Behavioral Artificial
   Intelligence Network
Dr. William Hutchinson
12820 Holdridge Rd.
Silver Spring, MD 20906

The Behavior Therapist
Association for the Advancement of
   Behavior Therapy
15 West 36 St.
New York, NY 10018

Periodicals

A+: The Independent Guide for
   Apple Computing
P.O. Box 2965
Boulder, CO 80322

Byte
30 Main St.
Peterborough, NH 03458
(603) 924-9281

Creative Computing
Ahl Computing, Inc.
3460 Wilshire Blvd.
Los Angeles, CA 90010

MAC World
PC World Communications, Inc.
555 DeHaro St.
San Francisco, CA 94107

Microcomputing
Wayne Screen, Inc.
80 Pine St.
Peterborough, NH 03458

PC World
PC World Communications, Inc.
555 DeHaro St.
San Francisco, CA 94107
(800) 247-5470

Nibble
Microsparc, Inc.
10 Lewis St.
Lincoln, MA 01773
(617) 259-9710

Popular Computing
70 Main St.
Peterborough, NH 03458
(603) 924-9281

Data-Base Service Publications

Directory of Fee-Based Information
   Services
Burwell Enterprises
Suite 349
5106 FM 1960 West
Houston, TX 77069

Getting On-Line
M. David Stone
Prentice-Hall
Englewood Cliffs, NJ 07632
(201) 592-2000

Specialized Software Vendors

Academic Software
25824 Dundee Rd.
Huntington Woods, MI 48070
(313) 547-3433

ASIEP Education Company
3216 N.E. 27th
Portland, OR 97212

American Guidance Service
Publishers' Building
Circle Pines, MN 55014
(800) 328-2560

Applied Innovations, Inc.
South Kingstown Office Park
Wakefield, RI 02879
(800) 272-2250

Jerome Blumenthal, M.D.
145 Riverside Dr.
Binghamton, NY 13905
(Billing)

Ideal Systems
P.O. Box 681, Dept. E.
Fairfield, IA 52556
(515) 472-4507

Integrated Professional Systems, Inc.
5211 Mahoning Ave.
Suite 135
Youngstown, OH 44515
(216) 799-3282

Medical Psychology Institute
566 South San Vincente Blvd.
Los Angeles, CA 90048

National Computer Systems
Professional Assessment Services,
  Dept. 303
P.O. Box 1416
Minneapolis, MN 55440
(800) 328-6759

Precision People, Inc.
3452 North Ride Circle. S.
Jacksonville, FL 32217
(904) 262-1096

Psychological Assessment Resources,
  Inc.
P.O. Box 98
Odessa, FL 33556
(813) 977-3395

Psychologistics, Inc.
P.O. Box 3896
Indialantic, FL 32903
(305) 259-7811

Psychometric Software, Inc.
2050 S. Patrick Dr.
Indian Harbour Beach, FL 32937
(305) 259-8134

PsychStar Software
2745 W. Hilts Rd.
Route 4
Gladwin, MI 48624
(517) 426-1451

PsyQ Systems
1730 Rhode Island Ave., N.W.
Suite 714
Washington, DC 20036
(202) 822-8881

Reason House
204 East Joppa Road
Penthouse Suite 10
Towson, MD 21204
(310) 321-7270

Speech Synthesis and Recognition

MCE, Inc.
157 S. Kalamazoo Mall
Kalamazoo, MI 49007
(616) 345-8681

The Micromint, Inc.
561 Willow Ave.
Cedarhurst, NY 11516
(800) 645-3479

Street Electronics Corporation
1140 Mark Ave.
Carpinteria, CA 93013
(805) 684-4593

Votrax, Inc.
1394 Rankin
Troy, MI 48084
(800) 521-1350

Miscellaneous

The Apple Guide to Personal
  Computers in Education
20525 Mariani Ave.
Cupertino, CA 95014
(408) 996-1010

Personal Computers and the
Disabled: A resource guide
Apple Computers, Inc.
20525 Mariani Ave.
Cupertino, CA 95014
(408) 996-1010

Robotics Age Product Guide
Robotics Age
174 Concord St.
Peterborough, NH 03458

SOFsearch International, Inc.
P.O. Box 5776
San Antonio, TX 78201
(800) 531-5955
(A service to aid in software selection.)

Index

About the Author

Raymond G. Romanczyk (PhD, Rutgers University, 1974) is currently Associate Professor of Psychology and Director of the Children's Unit for Treatment and Evaluation and the Children's Unit for Learning Disabilities, and is former Director of Clinical Training at SUNY-Binghamton. Dr. Romanczyk has written numerous research articles and chapters in the area of childhood disorders and treatment. He is on the editorial board of several journals and is software editor for *Analysis and Intervention in Developmental Disabilities*.

Stephanie Lockshin is a graduate student in the PhD Clinical Psychology program at SUNY-Binghamton, Binghamton, NY 13901.

Psychology Practitioner Guidebooks

Editors:
Arnold P. Goldstein, Syracuse University
Leonard Krasner, SUNY at Stony Brook
Sol L. Garfield, Washington University